# TWENTIETH CENTURY VIEWS

The aim of this series is to present the best in contemporary critical opinion on major authors, providing a twentieth century perspective on their changing status in an era of profound revaluation.

Maynard Mack, *Series Editor*
Yale University

# THOMAS WOLFE

## A COLLECTION OF CRITICAL ESSAYS

Edited by
*Louis D. Rubin, Jr.*

Prentice-Hall, Inc.  *Englewood Cliffs, N.J.*

A SPECTRUM BOOK

*Library of Congress Cataloging in Publication Data*

RUBIN, LOUIS DECIMUS
   Thomas Wolfe; a collection of critical essays.

   (Twentieth century views) (A Spectrum Book)
   Bibliography:  p.
   1. Wolfe, Thomas, 1900–1938.
PS3545.0337Z848     813'.5'2     73–7522
ISBN 0–13–961656–X
ISBN 0–13–961649–7 (pbk)

10  9  8  7  6  5  4  3  2  1

PRENTICE-HALL INTERNATIONAL, INC. (*London*)

PRENTICE-HALL OF AUSTRALIA PTY. LTD. (*Sydney*)

PRENTICE-HALL OF CANADA LTD. (*Toronto*)

PRENTICE-HALL OF INDIA PRIVATE LIMITED (*New Delhi*)

PRENTICE-HALL OF JAPAN, INC. (*Tokyo*)

Acknowledgment is gratefully made to the following, for their permission to reprint from the works of Thomas Wolfe:

To Charles Scribner's Sons, and William Heinemann Ltd, for quotations from
*Look Homeward, Angel* (copyright 1929 Charles Scribner's Sons; renewal copyright © 1957 Edward C. Aswell, Administrator, C.T.A. and/or Fred W. Wolfe).
*Of Time and the River* (copyright 1935 Charles Scribner's Sons; renewal copyright © 1963 Paul Gitlin, Administrator, C.T.A.).
*The Story of a Novel* (copyright 1936 Charles Scribner's Sons; renewal copyright © 1964 Paul Gitlin, Administrator, C.T.A.).

To Harper & Row, Publishers, Inc., and William Heinemann Ltd, for quotations from
*You Can't Go Home Again* (copyright 1934, 1937, 1938, 1939, 1940 by Maxwell Perkins as Executor; renewed 1968 by Paul Gitlin).

To Paul Gitlin, for quotations from the *Pocket Notebook*. All quotations from Wolfe's unpublished writings which appear in the present volume are made with the permission of the Administrator of the Estate of Thomas Wolfe, Mr. Paul Gitlin, 5 West 45th Street, New York, N.Y. Further quotation of these excerpts will require a similar grant of permission.

# Contents

For Jay and Ann Logan

*'Sauve qui peut'*

# Introduction: The Sense of Being Young

## by Louis D. Rubin, Jr.

### I.

There are writers who, in the way they interpret our experience for us and because of the circumstances in which we first happen upon them, exist in a special and personal relationship to us. Particularly when we are young and only beginning to discover the full resources of literature, we may, if we are lucky, come upon a writer who can speak to us so eloquently and so pointedly that he sets our imagination on fire. Thereafter, no matter how many books we read, or how much we later come to appreciate and admire other and sometimes better writers, the glow of that first one never quite wears off. And if we try to explain what it is about such a writer's books that makes them worth reading, we can never describe it in completely objective terms, for our experience has been so intense and so personal that when we talk about that writer and his work, in part at least we are talking about ourselves.

Thomas Wolfe might be described as a "writer's writer"—in particular, a young apprentice writer's writer. I do not mean by this what is usually meant by the phrase—that Wolfe's literary craftsmanship is such that other practitioners read him to see how well it can be done; far from it. My guess is that very, very few professional writers would think of turning to the fiction of Thomas Wolfe for instruction in the techniques of their art. Rather, what I find significant is the number of really good American writers who read Thomas Wolfe when they were young and first thinking about being

A portion of the text of this introduction was read at the annual meeting of the North Carolina Literary and Historical Association in December, 1972, and published under the title of "Thomas Wolfe Once Again" in the *North Carolina Historical Review* for Spring, 1973 (L, No. 2), pp. 169–89.

writers, and who drew from his books a sense of the dignity of writing and the determination to try it themselves. Some of these writers
ultimately became far more skilled practitioners of the craft of story-
telling than ever Wolfe was. But apparently what he was able to do
was to help them believe in the worthiness of their would-be voca-
tions, and to make them hope that they could indeed become good
writers. From the Wolfe novels they drew the inspiration of a young
man wanting to write, refusing to settle for the surface denotation
of American life, intent upon getting at its emotional dimensions.
William Faulkner's admiration for Wolfe, for example, is precisely
of this kind. Of his contemporaries, he once remarked, he valued
Wolfe most because he tried the hardest to say the most. "Man has
but one short life to write in," Faulkner said, "and of course he
wants to say it all before he dies. My admiration for Wolfe is that
he tried his best to get it all said; he was willing to throw away style,
coherence, all the rules of preciseness, to try to put all the experience
of the human heart on the head of a pin, as it were." [1] Faulkner was
careful to point out that he didn't think Wolfe succeeded in what
he was trying to do, but that the effort he made was what mattered.

It is this sense of Wolfe striving to tell it all, rocked by sensation
and emotion and searching for a way to articulate it, that has had
so profound an impact on so many young authors. Encountering
Wolfe, particularly if one is young and a would-be writer, has often
turned out to be not merely an event; it is an emotional experience.
It can mark a stage in the development of one's sensibilities, and one
remembers it ever afterward. There have been few American authors, I think, who have been capable of affording just this particular kind of intense experience. What Wolfe did was not merely to
dramatize the stories of his protagonists' lives; he also dramatized
his desire to tell about those lives. Nothing could be further from
Stephen Dedalus's (but not James Joyce's) theory of the invisible
artist, refined out of existence, indifferent, paring his fingernails,
than the Wolfe novels. The authorial personality that is Thomas
Wolfe is always visible, showing and then telling, vigorously but-
tressing his protagonist's consciousness with external authorial

---

[1] Quoted in Richard Walser, "Preface" to *The Enigma of Thomas Wolfe: Biographical and Critical Selections,* ed. Walser (Cambridge, Mass.: Harvard University Press, 1953), p. vii.

rhetoric. In a sense, all of Wolfe's novels are about the feelings of a young man who wants to write, and it is to this that so many of his readers have responded.

## II.

My own encounter with the Wolfe novels—if I may become confessional for a moment in order to make what I hope is an important point—has been a lifelong affair. I first came upon Thomas Wolfe in 1943, when I was 19 years old and a Private First Class in the Army of the United States. A year earlier, I had taken a course in "The Modern Novel" at college. The two "modern" novels we read were Samuel Butler's *The Way of All Flesh* and John Galsworthy's *The Forsyte Saga*. These books had been about the extent of my encounter with the twentieth-century literary imagination in fiction. To say that I was enthralled with Thomas Wolfe scarcely describes what happened. I read *Look Homeward, Angel,* and straightaway I was transported into a realm of literary experience that I had not known could exist. No writer, as Thoreau once remarked of Whitman, can communicate a new experience to us; but what he can do is to make us recognize the importance of our own experience, so that we become aware, for the first time, of what it is that we feel and think and what it can mean for us. This is what Thomas Wolfe did for me. He described a young man whose sensuous apprehension of life was matched by his appetite for feeling. Not only did he render the concrete details of experience in brilliant specificity, but he responded to the details lavishly and lyrically. Everything he thought, observed, and did was suffused with feeling. For a young reader such as myself there could be an instantaneous and quite exhilarating identification, not only with the youthful protagonist, Eugene Gant, but with the autobiographical author who was describing Eugene's experience with so much approval and pride. And it was on emotional response—not in its subtlety or discrimination, but in its intensity—that the highest premium was placed. What was depicted as most valuable and most real was the intensity with which one could apprehend and react. Beyond that, it was not fineness of discrimination or critical fastidiousness that counted; it was variety, range. With such a writer as this, the potentialities for new experience seemed endless. The sound of a streetcar, the motion of an express train, the look of a street, the smell of a waterfront, the bitterness of young love jilted—the hunger was for new modes and varieties, and the more of them the better.

Here was a writer who seemed to desire nothing less than to storm the gates of heaven in frontal assault. I read, in *Of Time and the River,* the description of Eugene Gant riding on a train, standing in the vestibule between the pullmans and letting the clamorous beat of wheels on the steel rail punctuate his joy at going northward. That was just the way I had felt, traveling on a train, but until then I had not thought it could be worthy of the dignity of literary utterance. Thomas Wolfe assured me that indeed it was, and that the emotional intensity that I was prone to bring to such moments was not only entirely appropriate, but a definite proof of superior sensibility. He subtitled his second novel "A Legend of Man's Hunger in His Youth," and not only did he delineate the hunger but—and this is of absolute importance—by thus depicting it in language he showed that it was worthwhile, since out of it art could be fashioned. It was not merely that Thomas Wolfe described, richly and in detail, the world of sensation, experience, and desire as it presented itself to a young man; he also made it quite clear how intensely the young man felt and thought about it, and, in so doing, confirmed in rhetoric the value of the youthful perspective. The autobiographical relationship was essential to the experience of reading him; you had to recognize the experience that he showed you, and you had to realize that in thus remembering it he was giving meaning to it in language —so that presumably, since you were able to see it in the same way, you too were capable of making it into something important. Now as a matter of fact this proposition was by no means self-evident; but the very example of the novels seemed to confirm it. What Wolfe was saying was that feeling counted for everything, and that if you could feel intensely enough about the things of your world, it was all the proof needed to know that you were virtuous.

It was the description, the concrete emotional evocation of the space and color and time of a young man's developing experience of himself and his world, that gave body to the Wolfe novels, anchored the rhetoric, and—for older and more experienced readers—ultimately helped to protect the art against the weakness of the rhetoric when, as sometimes in the early work and more frequently later, it tended to dissolve into empty assertion. But for myself when I first encountered him, and for many another like me, the rhetoric presented no problem at all. I welcomed it; and the more of it the better. In my own instance it was both an easy and an exhilarating experience to identify myself with the situation of *Look Homeward, Angel,* since I too was from a medium-sized city in the Carolinas, of a thoroughly middle-class background, and given in self-defense to viewing myself as a largely unappreciated and misunderstood devotee of Beauty and Truth in a society governed by adult philistinism and commerce. Thus the mode of the *Bildungsroman*—the growth and maturation of the sensitive young man—fitted my estimation of the situation quite comfortably, and in my instance there was little chance that Wolfe could go too far in describing and then praising Eugene Gant's romantic renunciation of the community's commercial ethos and the Gant family's failure to appreciate the hero's artistic talents. When I read Wolfe's statement that by the time Eugene Gant was 12 "he had learned by now to project mechanically, before the world, an acceptable counterfeit of himself which would protect him from intrusion," [2] I was enthralled with the recognition of a kindred sensibility, since that was exactly how I tended to view the matter.

Yet, as noted, ultimately it is the rhetoric that is the least satisfactory part of the Wolfe novels. Once the reader begins to suspect that they are special pleading, the extravagant justifications and assertions of virtue that constitute a goodly percentage of *Of Time and the River* and the two posthumously-published narratives come to pall, and the uncritical Wolfean hunger for quantity, without much concern for quality, begins after a while to seem tiresome. In *A Portrait of the Artist as a Young Man,* a book that obviously meant a great deal to Thomas Wolfe, James Joyce describes Stephen Dedalus as he lectures Lynch on aesthetics: "Stephen paused and, though his companion did not speak, felt that his words had called up around

---

[2] Thomas Wolfe, *Look Homeward, Angel* (New York: Modern Library, 1929), p. 201.

them a thoughtenchanted silence." [3] That is what Stephen thought; but it is not necessarily what James Joyce thought. However much the Joyce who wrote *A Portrait* may have admired his young artist's intensity of spirit and honesty of vision, clearly he was well aware of the difference between the emotional evaluation that his youthful protagonist gave to his experience, and the fact of an inexperienced and highly abstracted young artist *manqué* taking himself and his pronouncements with such uncritical gravity. Wolfe, by contrast, when it came down to what Eugene Gant felt was important, never admitted to there being any such difference; and he tried to buttress the autobiographical Eugene's evaluation with authorial rhetoric asserting that, By God, it was so, and that anyone who said it wasn't was an unfeeling philistine.

But this is not the crux of Wolfe's art. It is not the assertions of uniqueness and claims to special sensibility that constitute the primary strength of his fiction. William Styron, whose youthful first encounter with Wolfe was much like my own, writes of the shock of his "sudden exposure to a book like *Look Homeward, Angel,* with its lyrical torrent and raw, ingenuous feeling, its precise and often exquisite rendition of place and mood, its buoyant humor and the vitality of its characters"—and then he adds, "and, above all, the sense of youthful ache and promise and hunger and ecstasy which so corresponded to that of its eighteen-year-old reader . . ." [4] Thomas Wolfe was brilliantly able, for readers such as Styron and myself, to render the sense of being young. He did this in part with the rhetoric, to be sure—but most of all it was the world of experience that he opened up to vision. For a young man the world is apt to seem imminently there for the taking—and Thomas Wolfe portrayed it in glowing color and brilliant detail, shot full of emotional response. You had not realized that the Negro slum section of a Southern town could be described in prose so vividly that you might recognize it instantly. Wolfe took the mundane, the ordinary, the humdrum and recreated them so sharply in language that you saw them for almost the first time. Or rather, he drew together and articulated the dif-

[3] James Joyce, *A Portrait of the Artist as a Young Man* (New York: Viking Press, 1964), p. 213.

[4] William Styron, "The Shade of Thomas Wolfe," *Harper's,* CCXXXVI (April, 1968), p. 96.

fused and latent emotional impressions you had about something so that for the first time you recognized what you really saw and felt.


## III.


Wolfe's great subject, especially after *Look Homeward, Angel,* was America. He rendered it poetically, gave it a glamor and mystery, and made the places you were living in, and just beginning to explore, seem full of promise and excitement. As Styron says, "he was the first prose writer to bring a sense of America as a glorious abstraction, a vast and brooding continent whose untold bounties were waiting every young man's discovery . . ." And he goes on, "it was as if for the first time my whole being had been thrown open to the sheer *fertile* and *sensory* vividness of the American scene through which, until then, I had been walking numb and blind, and it caused me a thrill of discovery that was quite unutterable." [5]

Wolfe's "discovery of America," to which Styron alludes, has been the subject of much critical discussion and more than a little dispute. After *Look Homeward, Angel,* it did become for Wolfe not merely a process but a conscious theme, and one that, as Styron says, could enchant many readers. In *Look Homeward, Angel,* he sent Eugene Gant on a walk through downtown Altamont, and described dentist's offices, laundrywomen, undertaker's parlors, Y.M.C.A. secretaries, milliner's shops, and the like in a series of little vignettes of vivid color, and, concluded each with a quotation from a poem, as much as to say that in such mundane, everyday activities the same aesthetic response was appropriate as in the more literarily respectable objects depicted by the English poets. He ended up with a drugstore, and he made the soda fountain shine with the clarity and radiance usually reserved for Mermaid Taverns and the like. Citing a description of the Boston waterfront in *Of Time and the River* as an example of how Wolfe could invest American experience with glamor and excitement, Styron declares that it was after an immersion in Wolfe's America that he resolved himself to become a

[5] *Ibid.,* pp. 96, 98.

writer;[6] it is no accident that his own first novel opens with a scene on a train and its arrival at the Newport News waterfront.

No one could depict the excitement of a train trip with more excitement than Wolfe. The poetry of motion was his forte; it was not merely a matter of making a trip in order to arrive at this destination or that, but the experience of going for its own sake that enthralled him, and he portrayed it in a way that caught the imagination. Just why it was that travel on railroad trains so fascinated Wolfe, and also readers like myself, is not hard to discern. It was the voyage out, the escape from the confines of the known and bounded, the mundane circumstances of home and childhood. The powerful bulk of the locomotive—so much sound and fury, harnessed for full utilization of the energy while retaining its explosive glamor—swiftly bears the young Eugene Gant toward his destiny, in symbolism that is at once spiritual and materialistic, aesthetic and practical, selfless and highly sexual. " 'Do you know why you are going, or are you just taking a ride on the train?' " the ghost of Ben Gant asks Eugene just before Eugene is about to leave Altamont for the North. Eugene admits that he is not sure of his reasons, that " 'Perhaps I just want a ride on the train.' " [7] But if Eugene is unsure at that moment, both he and Thomas Wolfe are quite intent upon making the trip, and merely to be in motion is reason enough to go.

There are voyages in *Look Homeward, Angel,* but it is with *Of Time and the River* that they seem to become compulsive. Eugene travels to Baltimore and Boston, then back to Altamont, then down to South Carolina, then to New York, then on frequent train trips up the Hudson River and back again, then finally to Europe, where he visits first England, then Paris, then the south of France. At the end he is on the ship that will take him back across the ocean to the United States. Traveling, of course, is one way of possessing new experience through an act of the will—one boards the train, looks out the window, and new towns, new countryside, new scenes appear. In a fantasy Wolfe has Eugene imagine that the northbound train he is riding leaves the tracks and soars into space:

[6] *Ibid.*
[7] *Look Homeward, Angel,* p. 619.

To hell with Baltimore, New York, Boston! Run her off the Goddam rails! We're going West! Run her through the woods—cross fields—rivers, through the hills! Hell's pecker! But I'll shove her up the grade and through the gap, no doubleheader needed! Let's see the world now! Through Nebraska, boy! Let's shove her through, now, you can do it!—Let's run her through Ohio, Kansas, and the unknown plains! Come on, you hogger, let's see the great plains and the fields of wheat —Stop off in Dakota, Minnesota, and the fertile places—Give us a minute while you breathe to put our foot upon it, to feel it spring back with the deep elastic feeling, 8000 miles below, unrolled and lavish, depthless, different from the East.[8]

But of course there is a glass window between the viewer from the train and the life that goes on beyond the window, and the only human relationship thus acquired is that of an outsider, an on-looker. Many of the most moving lyrical passages in Wolfe's work after *Look Homeward, Angel* involve just such moments in which Eugene Gant, and less occasionally George Webber, look on people from a train window and recognize their kinship and their own loneliness. Such moments, however, are transitory; the human con-tact is limited to the momentary glimpse, whereupon the train moves on. As John Peale Bishop declares in an essay which though not basically favorable to Wolfe is one of the most understanding of all writings about him,

For a moment, but a moment only, there is a sudden release of com-passion, when some aspect of suffering and bewildered humanity is seized, when the other's emotion is in a timeless completion known. Then the moment passes, and compassion fails. For Eugene Gant, the only satisfactory relationship with another creature is one which can have no continuity. For the boy at the street corner, seen in the inde-cision of youthful lust, he has only understanding and pity; the train from which he looks moves on and nothing is required of Eugene. But if he should approach that same boy on the street, if he should come close enough to overhear him, he would hear only the defilement of language, words which would awaken in him only hate and disgust.[9]

[8] Thomas Wolfe, *Of Time and the River* (New York: Charles Scribner's Sons, 1935), p. 71.
[9] John Peale Bishop, "The Sorrows of Thomas Wolfe," in *The Collected Essays of John Peale Bishop*, ed. Edmund Wilson (New York: Charles Scribner's Sons), p. 135.

This, I take it, is in part what William Styron means in speaking of an abstract quality in Wolfe's America. On the one hand there is, especially in *Look Homeward, Angel* but often elsewhere as well, a portrayal of aspects of the American scene that is concrete, evocative, enormously *affective*. And there is also, in the work after the first novel, a deliberate and cumulative attempt to depict the idea of America itself—an attempt which, though involving much itemization and often long catalogues, is usually singularly impersonal in nature, in that the numerous specific items are chosen as typical examples rather than for themselves. The human contacts, in other words, are as viewed through a train window, and neither lasting nor individualized. Wolfe seeks to give them meaning through emotional rhetoric, the emotion belonging to his protagonist as he views them and to the novelist as he remembers viewing them. In page after page of *Of Time and the River* Eugene Gant is shown "experiencing" America, both while travelling across it and afterward through memory while in France. His longing for it while abroad is agonizing, his view of it as seen from train windows is full of love, compassion, desire. But when viewed in this way, as *America,* it consists entirely of lists, catalogues, assemblages of examples. It is, in other words, almost entirely quantitative, a collection of items, scenes, themes, names. There is little or no sorting out, no choosing of some of the items as more or less uniquely or typically American, more or less beautiful or meaningful, than others. And at the end what has been given is an abstraction, "America," along with a display of items that are proposed as typical examples of its makeup.

## IV.

It will not, however, suffice to leave the matter there. The passages and episodes in which Wolfe writes his long catalogues to express his protagonist's sense of America have another function. They serve that function imperfectly, and perhaps the method used to achieve it is not among the most efficient of available artistic strategies. But it is one that helps to account, in large part, for the tremendous impact that the Wolfe novels can make upon younger, romantically attuned readers. What the "America" episodes do is to dramatize both the Wolfean protagonist's and, importantly, the authorial personality's yearning for experience. The very fact that the emotional hunger is there, in such abundance, and that it cannot quite make contact with—or, to continue the metaphor, find adequate spiritual nourishment in—the substance at which it is being so urgently directed is itself a device for imaging the sense of loneliness and spiritual yearning that lies at the heart of the experience of reading the novels. And we go wrong, I think, if we refuse to accept that dimension, and dismiss such a viewpoint as an example of the so-called "imitative fallacy." For the experience of fiction is a subtle and complex affair, and if we try to leave out the "rhetoric" of the art, the formal function of the presence of the storyteller in our reading of the story he is telling, we may impoverish our relationship with a work of fiction.

What I am getting at is that in his fiction, especially in his earlier fiction, Wolfe *dramatizes himself as author,* warts and all. Or more precisely, he dramatizes himself in the act of looking at himself. What is involved here is not just a biographical matter, but also a formal, literary relationship. Not only is Wolfe's protagonist a dramatized version of himself when a bit younger, but the rhetoric of the interpretative description serves to set up a myself-when-younger relationship between the storyteller and the protagonist.

For example, in *Of Time and the River* Eugene Gant is at Harvard, studying drama, and he receives a telegram summoning him home to the bedside of his father, who is dying. He borrows money for the train fare, hurries to the South Station, boards a train, and watches from the window as it moves out of the station:

> Then the great train, gathering now in speed, and mounting smoothly to the summit of its tremendous stroke, was running swiftly through the outskirts of the city, through suburbs and brief blurs of light and then through little towns and on into the darkness, the wild and secret loneliness of earth. And he was going home again into the South and to a life that had grown strange as dreams, and to his father who was dying and who had become a ghost and shadow of his father to him, and to the bitter reality of grief and death. And—how, why, for what reason he could not say—all he felt was the tongueless swelling of wild joy. It was the wild and secret joy that has no tongue, the impossible hope that has no explanation, the savage, silent, and sweet

exultancy of night, the wild and lonely visage of the earth, the imperturbable stroke and calmness of the everlasting earth, from which we have been derived, wherein again we shall be compacted, on which all of us have lived alone as strangers, and across which, in the loneliness of night, we have been hurled onward in the projectile flight of mighty trains—America.[10]

The last, lengthy sentence, though it begins in the past tense—"It *was* the wild and secret joy . . ."— shifts the center of experience away from Eugene's sudden trip homeward and into the time of writing, in which the author, no longer the homeward-bound Eugene of the past, interprets what the joy *is*. Eugene, riding homeward from Boston on the train, first felt the joy; the authorial voice telling us about it recreates the moment; and how he feels about it as he describes it is precisely how Eugene felt when he experienced it. The aesthetic and emotional distance between Eugene going home and the author describing it is all but obliterated by the author's rhetoric, which bridges and unites the two experiences. With his rhetoric he injects himself into the narrative, ends up speaking directly to us, and the story becomes, as it has been doing from almost the first page onward, almost as much a demonstration of the recreating storyteller's sensibilities as an account of the protagonist Eugene Gant's youthful adventures.

This dual identity as both character and chronicler, enforced through rhetoric and attitude, is both the strength and the weakness of the Wolfe books. It enables Wolfe to bring to bear on his youthful protagonist's experience the impressive powers of his rhetoric. He can recognize, explore, and delineate the particularities of that experience. He can use the affective possibilities of rhetoric to intensify the meaning of the experience, and guide our response to it. He can, in other words, both show and persuade. Because the persuasion is coming from a formally established point of view, a recreating authorial personality who has convinced us, through his intimacy with the protagonist and his thoughts, that what is happening is important to him and also that its importance is *that* it happened to him, what he says about it takes on an authority that would otherwise be lacking if it were merely arbitrary authorial embellishment.

But just as surely, it can work that way only if we are willing to

[10] *Of Time and the River*, p. 246.

believe in the validity of both the youthful protagonist's experience
and the recreating interpreter's delineation of its importance. If ever
we feel that what the speaker tells us about the meaning of what
happened is exaggerated, or confused, or actually inaccurate, the
whole relationship breaks down. For the rhetorical stance of this
remembering sensibility has got to be plausible, too. When the
author says that Eugene did or thought such and such, we accept
that; but when he insists that what Eugene did or thought signifies
this or that about human experience, and we believe that it doesn't
so signify, he is in trouble; and when he tries to enforce his interpretation by cascades of affective rhetoric, what results is something
very different from what he intends. Let me cite another example,
from the material posthumously published as a novel, *The Web and
the Rock*. Wolfe is describing young George Webber's feelings and
behavior at a time when he has been quarreling with his mistress.
His novel has been rejected, he is in bad shape emotionally, and
sometimes, when he telephones his mistress's home to find her not in,
he imagines that Esther is betraying him.

> And he would leave the phone to drain the bottle to its last raw
> drop, then rush out in the streets to curse and fight with people, with
> the city, with all life, in tunnel, street, saloon, or restaurant, while the
> whole earth reeled about him its gigantic and demented dance.
> And then, in the crowded century of darkness that stretched from
> light to light, from sunset until morning, he would prowl a hundred
> streets and look into a million livid faces seeing death in all of them,
> and feeling death everywhere he went. He would be hurled through
> tunnels to some hideous outpost of the mighty city, the ragged edge of
> Brooklyn, and come out in the pale grey light of morning in a waste-
> land horror of bare lots and rust and rubbish; of dismal little houses
> flung rawly down upon the barren earth, joined each to each in blocks
> that duplicated one another with an idiot repetition.[11]

Here there are two levels of experience. One is that of George
Webber in love, as he suspects his mistress and suffers. However, by
use of the conditional tense—George "*would* leave the phone to
drain the bottle," and "*would* prowl a hundred streets," and "*would
be* hurled through tunnels"—the author makes it clear that the ex-

[11] Thomas Wolfe, *The Web and the Rock* (New York: Harper and Brothers,
1939), pp. 554–55.

perience is one that happened to George on characteristic occasions, rather than just the time being described. Clearly, therefore, it is the authorial personality who is speaking to us, recapitulating and summarizing his protagonist's experience over a period of time. Now presumably what the author is doing is showing us how it was with young George Webber at a bad time. It is not that Esther Jack is really betraying George; rather, George, in his pain and torment, imagines that she is, and on such occasions goes off like a madman into the night to wander about the city in his anguish. Under such conditions, his behavior could hardly be termed inexplicable. Nor would it be improbable that at such a time, drunk, distraught, despondent, George might well envision the city through which he is wandering in just such fashion as described. But exactly who is it that sees the walk as a "prowl" along "a hundred streets," during which George looks "into a million livid faces seeing death in all of them"? To whom does "the ragged edge of Brooklyn" appear as "some hideous outpost," as "a wasteland horror of bare lots and rust and rubbish," and of "dismal little houses flung rawly down upon the barren earth"? Is it the distraught young protagonist, or the supposedly more objective authorial personality who interprets what happened? The answer, both syntactically and emotionally, is that both of them see and evaluate it that way. As with the train trip, there is thus little or no difference between the two perspectives. At such moments, all too frequent after *Look Homeward, Angel,* the reader is likely to refuse to accept the interpretation of George Webber's experience that the author insists upon. He can go along with the notion that young George Webber may have felt that way about the city at the time, and that George may indeed have imagined that he was prowling a hundred streets and looking into a million livid faces, but when the storyteller, the remembering author who as interpreter and judge ought not still to feel betrayed and overcome with a sense of failure, also interprets and evaluates the experience in that fashion, without irony or humor or reservation of any sort, it is something else again. The sympathy and understanding that the reader might have for the youthful George Webber at such times of torment is seriously undercut when he realizes that the author is in complete agreement with his protagonist, that he sees nothing excessive, nothing pathological, nothing childish or histrionic in

George's attitude, but is recounting it with complete approval and endorsement.

## V.

The experience of Thomas Wolfe's fiction, therefore, involves two factors. One is the way in which the doings of the protagonists of the novels are described and communicated to us. The other is the way in which the authorial voice interprets and evaluates those doings. But these two factors cannot be separated from each other and considered in isolation. The impact of the first, as we have seen, is made possible in part by the second. The success of *Look Homeward, Angel* is based on the rich, emotion-laden concreteness of the characterizations of the Gant family and especially of Eugene, and it is the presence of the remembering author that makes them possible. *Look Homeward, Angel* had not the focus upon and through the apprentice artist-protagonist's consciousness alone that we find in Joyce's *A Portrait of the Artist as a Young Man*; we see the Gant family before Eugene is born, and throughout there are frequent chapters devoted to W. O. Gant, Eliza, and others of the family, which are not part of the youthful Eugene's experience at all. But it is the remembering artist's recreation and interpretation that unifies the novel. When W. O. Gant comes back from his western trip in Chapter 7, there is no way that his infant son Eugene can know what is going on in his mind; but the fact that the son is, as remembering author, recreating what went on in his father's mind gives this Joycean chapter a double function in the novel—it tells what manner of person W. O. Gant is as man and father, and it helps to forward our developing awareness of the sensibility of the remembering storyteller as he recreates his past for us. The technique that Wolfe uses here is based very largely on the treatment of Bloom in Chapters IV–VI of Joyce's *Ulysses*—we look into W. O. Gant's mind, observe through his eyes and then watch his thinking about what he sees, but we also view Gant from the outside, as the author wishes us to see him. Wolfe calls him "Gant the Far-Wanderer," and tells us what he does in a way that Gant himself could not do. And toward the end of the episode Wolfe does what Joyce does not do in those particular chapters (though he does something like it later in *Ulysses*): he thrusts his own authorial voice directly into the narrative to explain, in his own language, what W. O. Gant and, briefly, Eliza, are doing and thinking, and what it means. The episode finally ends up being fitted into the sensibility and the consciousness of the remembering storyteller, and it draws its ultimate significance in the novel from what that remembering storyteller can make of it. At the end of the novel, the fact that the protagonist is about to turn away from the place where all this has happened, and that as experience it is concluded for him, combines with the fact of the reader's knowledge that what he has been reading is a recreation and ordering of what has happened, to give the novel its conclusion and its meaning.

The early reviews of *Look Homeward, Angel* all remark on the vividness of the characterization of the Gant family and on the presence, throughout, of the sense of loneliness and lostness. The latter is not so much there because of what the characters themselves say and think as because the remembering author keeps interpreting their experience in that way and keeps stressing that quality. And, by and large, it works. The reader is willing to accept that rhetorical interpretation. The loneliness of a young man, the sadness over the dissolution of his family in time, the sense of deprivation and loss— these are not inappropriate or extraneous to the experience being described. And if, to a reader unable to take the emotions of the adolescent Eugene Gant with quite the seriousness that the author does, the importance placed on Eugene's sensibility in the latter chapters begins to seem a bit overdone, there is still enough vivid experience in *Look Homeward, Angel,* and enough believable emotional content in the rhetorical interpretation by the narrator, to make this book an impressive, original work of art. One may weary of the incessant reiteration of the *O lost!* motif, may come to feel that Eugene Gant's loneliness is being insisted on too stridently, but it is the reiteration, and not the attitude itself, that is overdone. The author, that is, may be using his rhetoric to exaggerate the attitudes he is expressing, but the attitudes are believable. Generally, the reader can feel that what the rhetoric says the story means is what the story does mean, even if overstated and insisted upon too fervently.

With *Of Time and the River,* however, it is another matter. To guide us in our apprehension of Eugene's post-Altamont adventures we get, in Wolfe's second novel, a great deal more authorial rhetoric than was previously offered. Not only is *Of Time and the River* a much longer book than *Look Homeward, Angel,* but it also contains far more direct assertion by the author. In his famous critical attack on Wolfe, "Genius Is Not Enough," the late Bernard DeVoto objected to what he called all the "placental material" in the novels. There had been a good deal of such material in *Look Homeward, Angel,* he said, along with some fiction of altogether superb quality. But in *Of Time and the River* the placental material had taken over, and in addition had been given a rationalization: it was supposed to connote the "voiceless and unknown womb of Time" and of "dark and lonely and lost America." This writing which DeVoto termed placental, and which he felt should have been discarded en route to the story itself, was no more and no less than the authorial rhetoric, which DeVoto described as "long, whirling discharges of words, unabsorbed in the novel, unrelated to the proper business of fiction, badly if not altogether unacceptably written, raw gobs of emotion, aimless and quite meaningless jabber, claptrap, belches, grunts, and Tarzanlike screams." [12] But while many readers will agree with the burden of DeVoto's strictures, that *Of Time and the River* is an overwritten and unstructured book that would have profited greatly by a great deal more cutting and revising than the author was willing to give it, it should be recognized that DeVoto's memorable assault fails to comprehend how the Wolfe novels actually work as fiction. DeVoto's theory of fiction dismissed absolutely what we have seen to be a necessary dimension of the art of fiction as practiced by Wolfe—that conscious presence of the authorial voice interpreting the doing of the protagonist. "A novel *is*—it cannot be asserted, ranted, or even detonated," DeVoto said. "A novelist represents life. When he does anything else, no matter how beautiful or furious or ecstatic the way in which he does it, he is not writing fiction." [13] But the truth is that a novelist can, if he is good enough, use all those methods and yet be representing life in so doing. For

[12] Bernard DeVoto, "Genius Is Not Enough," *Saturday Review of Literature,* XIII (April 25, 1936), pp. 3–4.
[13] *Ibid.,* p. 14.

part of the representing—in Aristotelian terms, the imitation—happens to be the act of giving order and meaning, and when Wolfe uses his authorial rhetoric to reinforce, interpret, comment upon his protagonist's actions and thoughts, we object not when the rhetoric as such shows up, but only as it fails to enhance our interpretation and evaluation of what the protagonist's life means. When it does fit the occasion, when what the authorial personality says about the protagonist seeems believable and appropriate, then, far from being disconcerted by the presence of the rhetoric, we accept it and let it help us to take part in the experience of the fiction. What I think DeVoto really objected to, though he did not understand it, was not the asserting, ranting, or detonating rhetoric, but the inappropriateness of such rhetoric as an accurate and believable interpretation of the experience being chronicled. When Wolfe goes off on a long lyrical flight about Eugene's train trip northward as representing the soul of America, and the interpreting narrator poeticizes for pages about what Eugene Gant is doing and feeling, it isn't the rhetorical presence at such that annoys, but the sense that the author is attempting to exaggerate the emotional ardor of the youthful, drunken Eugene Gant into a triumphant rhapsodic insistence upon the poetic virtue of Eugene's superior sensibility. We can't and don't believe that the experience signifies or proves all that; and the more the author goes on about it the less convincing he seems.

The intense experience that reading Wolfe can be for the young, I think, is possible precisely because of the ability and the willingness of a certain kind of younger reader to accept, at face value and as a version of the truth, just the signification that the narrator is attaching to it. This reader identifies with the author. For him a rhetorical exercise such as that involving the spirit of America isn't at all "placental"; rather, it is an important part of the experience of reading *Of Time and the River,* because it pronounces the meaning and significance of the train trip, and reinforces the feelings of the younger Eugene Gant who made the trip with the more "mature" rhetorical approval of the author telling about it. The book works by an alternation of viewpoint between the younger Eugene and his older writing self, in which the younger man acts and feels and thinks and then the older man not only expresses his approval but confirms the verdict in emotive rhetoric. The charm, for the younger reader, lies in the fact that although the older, commenting narrator is, by dint of his rhetorical skill and the obvious fact that he wrote the book, no mere youth first undergoing the experience, he nevertheless not only accepts and ratifies the younger viewpoint but extols it as being even more significant than the younger protagonist himself had realized. The verve, the self-importance, the romantic insistence upon uniqueness of sensibility, the essentially uncritical, quantitative hunger for sensation of the adolescent and post-adolescent, free of qualification or ironic presentation by the older narrator, are enthusiastically received by many younger readers. My own copy of *Of Time and the River* is dated 1944, when I was twenty; it is the copy that I used a little more than a year later when I gave a report on Wolfe in an English class I was enrolled in after the war was over, and its margins are marked to indicate the passages I chose for reading aloud on that occasion: almost uniformly they were those with the greatest amount of rhetorical bombast, the most enraptured expressions of loneliness and exhilaration, the most arrogant and impassioned assertions of uniqueness and superior sensibility. Clearly the rhetoric did not faze me; obviously I considered those rhapsodic catalogues, that now seem so empty and self-deceiving, to be profound statements about the nature of reality. Here, for example, is a passage I marked from the train episode early in *Of Time and the River*:

What is it that we know so well and cannot speak? What is it that we want to say and cannot tell? What is it that keeps swelling in our hearts its grand and solemn music, that is aching in our throats, that is pulsing like a strange wild grape through all the conduits of our blood, that maddens us with its exultant and intolerable joy and that leaves us tongueless, wordless, maddened by our fury to the end?

We do not know. All that we know is that we lack a tongue that could reveal, a language that could perfectly express the wild joy swelling to a music in our heart, the wild pain welling to a strong ache in our throat, the wild cry mounting to a madness in our brain, the thing, the word, the joy we know so well, and cannot speak! All that we know is that the little stations whip by in the night, the straggling little towns whip by with all that is casual, rude, familiar, ugly, and unutterable. All that we know is that the earth is flowing by us in the darkness, and that this is the way the world goes—with a field and a

wood and a field! And of the huge and secret earth all we know is that
we feel with all our life its texture with our foot upon it.[14]

Why those sentences appealed to me when I was one-and-twenty, I
can only dimly surmise now. For one thing, they assert that the condition of very young manhood is one of a tremendous urgency of
feeling and emotion, and that the cause, the locus, of such feeling is
essentially indefinable. Furthermore, and most important, they assert that there is really no need to have to understand and define
it, for the feeling itself is all that matters. The passage is violently
and highly romantic; it predicates, as the norm, an infinite capacity
for feeling, without any real need at all for attempting to understand
the nature of the feeling, or any necessity for the feeling being
grounded in an object or a situation. There is no requirement that
the emotion be used, no suggestion that until or unless it is made
part of the design and purpose of one's life, it will remain unan-
chored, useless, and ineffective. Quite the contrary; it insists that "all
that we know" is the intensity of the emotion itself. The implication
is clearly that any attempt to make anything more or different of it
than that would be to cheapen the emotion.

Now to have someone say that, to say it in words that pile up one
upon the other in a massive rhetorical progression that reproduces
the vague but intense feeling being described, is quite likely to have
a powerful appeal for a young person who thinks he can recognize in
it his own portrait, done largely as he likes to conceive of himself. It
is this that accounts for the tremendous feeling of identification
that so many younger readers have with the Wolfe novels and their
author. It is indeed the "shock of recognition" that is involved: the
discovery that one's inmost feelings have been articulated by another,
so that presumably they are worth having after all.

But the trouble with such feelings, as James Joyce recognized
about the young Stephen Dedalus, is that that is all they are: un-
anchored, unused and, in their present form, unusable emotion.
In the diary that culminates *A Portrait of the Artist as a Young
Man,* Stephen records, for 10 April, a rhapsodic passage about the
sound of hoofs on the road, but on 11 April he records "Read what
I wrote last night. Vague words for a vague emotion." [15] There are

---

[14] *Of Time and the River,* p. 34.
[15] Joyce, *A Portrait of the Artist,* p. 251.

no such passages as that latter entry in the litanies of Eugene Gant, for there is no such qualitative distance between Eugene Gant and Thomas Wolfe; the young man's attitude toward his own importance is fully endorsed by the somewhat older novelist writing about him. Wolfe seems to have had none of Joyce's Thomistic zeal for precise signification, none of Joyce's insistence upon defining his terms. The difference, to be sure, is not always in Joyce's favor. Placed alongside Eugene Gant's sensuous apprehension of his experience in *Look Homeward, Angel,* the emotional apprehension of life of Stephen Dedalus in *A Portrait* seems impoverished, narrow. But what for a boy and a very young man is appropriate and in its way even admirable becomes for an adult something less than that. We will allow, even encourage, the youth and the young man to go after his experience hungrily, uncritically; later on will be time enough to sort things out and decide which parts of it he wishes to use. But when the young man moves on into full adulthood, and it is time for his emotional apprenticeship to be done with, we grow impatient with a continued refusal to sort out, criticize, choose and select; as DeVoto put it, "if the death of one's father comes out emotionally even with a ham-on-rye, then the art of fiction is cockeyed." [16] The difficulty for the adult reader of the Wolfe novels, in particular after *Look Homeward, Angel,* is that not only does the autobiographical protagonist insist upon holding on to his immaturity, but the interpreting author equally insists upon the entire appropriateness of his doing so and upon the spiritual insensitivity of all who refuse to go along with him when he does it. Furthermore, the authorial commentator, for all his approval, appears to become increasingly apprehensive that others may not share his approbation, and his response is to double and treble his own rhetorical assertion of the rightness of Eugene's behavior, attempting to sweep away all possible objections, including perhaps his own, in a torrent of words. This is the material that DeVoto calls placental. It is not that, so much as simply superfluous. It has nothing to do with unformed stuff out of which fiction should be made; it is not unprocessed, and unrealized, but misdirected and repetitiously expended.

[16] DeVoto, "Genius Is Not Enough," p. 4.

## VI.

If Wolfe had lived to revise the material published as his last two novels, would he as a writer have changed in any significant way? Was he working, as some have claimed, toward a much greater maturity and objectivity—toward the social rather than the lyrical novel? One is not at all sure. In 1938, after Wolfe had broken with Maxwell Perkins and Charles Scribner's Sons and had signed a contract with Harper and Brothers, he wrote his new editor, Edward C. Aswell, about the plans for his new book. The choice of the protagonist, he informed Aswell, would be crucial. He was done with "lyrical and identifiable personal autobiography" such as had characterized his first two novels:

> In other words, the value of the Eugene Gant type of character is his personal and romantic uniqueness, causing conflict with the world around him: in this sense, the Eugene Gant type of character becomes a kind of romantic self-justification, and the greatest weakness of the Eugene Gant type of character lies in this fact.
>
> Therefore, it is first of all vitally important to the success of this book that there be no trace of Eugene Gant-i-ness in the character of the protagonist, and since there is no longer a trace of Eugene Gant-i-ness in the mind and spirit of the creator, this problem should be a technical one rather than a spiritual or emotional one. In other words, this is a book about discovery, and not about self-justification . . .[17]

All this sounds very good, but when Wolfe proceeds to tell Aswell what it is that he intends to do, it turns out that the main change he has in mind will be to make his new protagonist a short, stocky, long-limbed man rather than a tall one, and that in the course of the narrative he will learn to accept his physical variance from the norm. And after he describes the prologue he will write, he goes on to say that the narrative itself will begin in a railroad station:

> For the purpose of this beginning—this setting—is to show the tremendous and nameless Allness of the Station—ten thousand men and

[17] Letter, Thomas Wolfe to Edward C. Aswell, February 14, 1938, in Elizabeth Nowell ed., *The Letters of Thomas Wolfe* (New York: Charles Scribner's Sons, 1956), p. 714.

women constantly arriving and departing, each unknown to the other, but sparked with the special fire of his own destination, the unknown town, the small hand's breadth of earth somewhere out on the vast body of the continent—all caught together for a moment, interfused and interweaving, not lives but life, caught up, subsumed beneath the great roof of the mighty Station, the vast murmur of these voices drowsily caught up there like the murmurous and incessant sound of time and of eternity, which is and is forever, no matter what men come and go through the portals of the great Station, no matter what men live or die.[18]

Will the new work, then, really be very different from what has come before? Is the Eugene Gant-i-ness really banished, both from the protagonist and from the mind of the creator? One doubts it. For what lies at the center of the Eugene Gant-i-ness, and gives it its special quality, is not the youthful protagonist's romantic self-justification, so much as the authorial storyteller's. It has been the remembering narrator's inability to distinguish his perspectives from those of his autobiographical protagonist's, and his insistence upon asserting, in pyramiding rhetoric, the validity and the wisdom of his protagonist's view of himself, that has given the first two novels the quality of youthful self-justification. And nothing in what Wolfe wrote about his future work gives much indication that the author's attitude toward his autobiographical protagonist will be significantly more distanced than with the earlier work. He still envisions his protagonist as existing at the center of the universe. What is important about the railroad station, he says, is "not lives but life"—which, since his protagonist is going to be in the station, means that the protagonist's experience will be thought of by the narrator as absolutely archetypal, possessing the significance of Everyman. Not for a moment does it occur to him that his protagonist's experience may possibly be less than that, that it may be one man's life only, not Life in general. An unkind critic, reading that outline, might well remark that the arrogance of seeing one's protagonist as archetypal is fully as arrogant as that of seeing him as unique.

So I doubt that toward the end of his career Thomas Wolfe was moving convincingly away from that romantic self-justification, and that the books he would have written had he lived would have been

[18] *Ibid.*, p. 719.

importantly less egocentric than his earlier work. Indeed, the single clue I see toward any such eventuality ever occurring lies not in his posthumously-published fictions, which are more or less the same thing as before, but in one sentence in the last thing he ever wrote, the letter penned to Maxwell Perkins on August 12, 1938, from the hospital in Seattle during his final illness. Writing at a time when he thought he had a chance for recovery, though he knew he was critically ill, he told his first editor that "so much of mortality still clings to me—I wanted most desperately to live and still do, and I thought about you all a thousand times, and wanted to see you all again, and there was the impossible anguish and regret of all the work I had not done, of all the work I had to do—and I know now I'm just a grain of dust, and I feel as if a great window has been opened on life I did not know about before—and if I come through this, I hope to God I am a better man, and in some strange way I can't explain, I know I am a deeper and a wiser one." [19]

"I know now I'm just a grain of dust . . ."—not "Man is just a grain of dust," but that one man, Thomas Wolfe, is: here we have a note different from anything found in any of the millions of words published or unpublished that Wolfe had written up to that time. Whether, if he had lived, that note would have been developed and sustained, we shall never know, for in just over a month's time, at the age of 37, he was dead.

## VII.

What we have in the Wolfe fiction, then, is the dramatized record of a talented and romantic young writer's encounter with the experience of being an artist in America, as it forced itself upon him. He described it happening, and he told us what he thought it meant. Especially after his first book, what he said it meant is often not what we think it really did mean, but there can be no mistaking the earnestness with which he presented his case, or questioning the artistic honesty of the attempt. We may disagree with the interpretation, may feel sometimes that he is trying to justify what cannot and

[19] Thomas Wolfe to Maxwell E. Perkins, August 12, 1938, in Nowell ed., *Letters of Thomas Wolfe*, p. 777.

should not be justified, and sometimes even that he is using his rhetoric to persuade himself as well as the reader. But let this be said: he never spares himself, never hides behind cheap deceits or clever, modish poses. His aim, as Faulkner says, was to tell it all, and though by no means always sure of what it was that he was telling, he did his best. This is why it seems to me that even *Of Time and the River,* for all its excess and its attitudinizing, comes out a pretty good book. We may not like all of what we see in it, but there can be no doubt that we have experienced something very formidable and very honest. What we have experienced is Thomas Wolfe trying to tell about himself as Eugene Gant; and I submit that this is worth having, and that we should let no theory of the effaced narrator prevent us from recognizing that this is the formal experience of the encounter with *Of Time and the River.* What one may think about the experience may change a great deal over the decades, but there can be no doubt that the transaction is there to be read: the story of the archetypal young American would-be artist, grotesqueries, awkwardness, self-deceptions and all, in search of his subject. Those who have dismissed that search as mere fustian—DeVoto, Clifton Fadiman, Stanley Hyman, Randall Jarrell, Caroline Gordon, John Donald Wade, many others—may have deprived themselves of a precious experience. One is moved to quote what the great artist Elstir says in Proust's *Within A Budding Grove,* when the young Marcel asks him, in effect, whether he was once the foolish little painter who had frequented the salon of the Verdurians:

"There is no man," he began, "however wise, who has not at some period of his youth said things, or lived in a way the consciousness of which is so unpleasant to him in later life that he would gladly, if he could, expunge it from his memory. And yet he ought not entirely to regret it, because he cannot be certain that he has indeed become a wise man—so far as it is possible for any of us to be wise—unless he has passed through all the fatuous or unwholesome incarnations by which that ultimate stage must be preceded. . . . We are not provided with wisdom, we must discover it for ourselves, after a journey through the wilderness which no one else can take for us, an effort which no one can spare us, for our wisdom is the point of view from which we come at last to regard the world. . . . I can see that the picture of what we once were, in early youth, may not be recognisable and cannot, certainly, be pleasing to contemplate in later life. But we must not deny the truth of it, for it is evidence that we have really lived. . . ." [20]

For many readers such as myself, the glory of Thomas Wolfe, I think, is that he can still show us that.

This thought arises, however. Granted that Wolfe could be what he was for Styron's generation and mine, is it still that way for today's young readers? Are there, indeed, any more provinces from which the journey outward could have the kind of significance it had for us? Does that special quality of guilelessness still exist among young people today, that allowed us to respond so confidently to what Wolfe was saying to us? I am not sure. I have the impression that fewer of my present students have read the Wolfe novels than was so even as late as a decade ago, and this even though I now teach at the very university that Wolfe and Eugene Gant attended and which is described in several of the novels. I wonder whether a generation that can respond to books such as Golding's *Lord of the Flies* and Percy's *The Last Gentleman* in the way that my present students can, could manage the invincible belief in personal potentiality that would seem to have been necessary to read Wolfe as an earlier generation once read him.

Yet I do know students, and good ones, who talk about Wolfe in much the same terms that we once did. Perhaps there are fewer of them, but they do indeed exist, and in sufficient numbers to make one think that it would be foolhardy to write the Wolfe novels off as artifacts in early twentieth-century literary history. And though the university I teach at is in the South, where the innocence might be thought to have lingered on a little longer than in more thoroughly metropolitan places, I note that not a few of the students who still respond to Wolfe are from the urban Northeast, and not the South at all. So I rather suspect that Eugene Gant will have his admirers for awhile yet. Apparently there are still a lot of us spiritual provincials left.

[20] Marcel Proust, *Remembrance of Things Past,* translated by C. K. Scott Moncrieff (New York: Random House, 1934), I, 649.

## VIII.

I have said little, in the remarks that have gone before, about the two posthumously published novels, *The Web and the Rock* and *You Can't Go Home Again*. This is to say in effect that I have said nothing about the problem of the Wolfe texts. In 1961 and 1962, almost a quarter-century after Wolfe's death, two books were published that together have had and will continue to have a profound impact upon his ultimate reputation and place in the American literary canon. These were *The Short Novels of Thomas Wolfe*, edited by C. Hugh Holman, and *The Window of Memory*: *The Literary Career of Thomas Wolfe*, by Richard S. Kennedy. Professor Kennedy, in an exhaustive study of the mass of Wolfe papers and manuscripts deposited at Harvard University, demonstrated what up until then had been only dimly realized even by the most assiduous of Wolfe scholars: that the two novels published as having been left by Thomas Wolfe after his death were in fact no such thing, but a massive scissors-and-paste job put together by Edward C. Aswell, Wolfe's second and last editor. To be sure, Aswell had indicated elsewhere that he had combined manuscript written at various stages throughout the last decade of Wolfe's life, but it had been generally assumed by everyone that Wolfe had designed the material as a more or less continuous narrative, and that Aswell had done little more than divide it into two books, eliminate overlappings and inconsistencies, and—for *You Can't Go Home Again*—add a few italicized transitional paragraphs when Wolfe had not provided them. What Kennedy showed was that not only had Aswell's editing been far more extensive than that, but he had virtually put together and published as two "novels" selections from a huge mass of disparate and fragmentary material not necessarily written as parts of such larger units at all. It had been Wolfe's intention to rewrite much of the material into a single narrative, and he had left a letter outlining the plan he had in mind, but in no real sense had the narrative ever actually existed. As Holman showed in his introduction (reprinted in this collection) to *The Short Novels of Thomas Wolfe*, much of that material had been written as short, independent works of fiction, designed and meant to stand by themselves, and, for that matter, already published as unitary works in various periodicals. Thus the "novels" supposedly written "by Thomas Wolfe" and published and sold as *The Web and the Rock* and *You Can't Go Home Again* could not properly be considered, in their published form, to be Wolfe's work. Furthermore, by publishing the short novels, Holman demonstrated that much of what had been assumed about Thomas Wolfe's literary imagination, and indeed about the very nature of his art, was in need of revision. For the Wolfe of the years following the publication of *Look Homeward, Angel* was not by nature a composer of big, untidy epics, but of shorter, much more shaped and patterned fictional forms.

Nor was this all. Kennedy showed what had been hinted at but nobody had ever really understood—that even *Of Time and the River* in the form in which it was published had not represented Wolfe's own way of telling it. Wolfe had written almost everything in it in the first person, and it was his editors who, with his reluctant consent, had gone through the manuscript and changed all the I's to he's! In addition, some of that material too had been written as shorter units, and it had been at the urging of Maxwell Perkins, Wolfe's first editor, that Wolfe had not followed *Look Homeward, Angel* with two shorter novels (one of which had even been partially set in type) but had waited six years in order to produce another novel of the scale of the first one.

In 1936, in his little book *The Story of a Novel,* Wolfe had described his great reliance upon Perkins's editorial guidance in deciding upon the form that *Of Time and the River* was to take, and he had been harshly criticized for such reliance, notably by DeVoto in "Genius is Not Enough." But no one had understood, until Kennedy furnished the evidence, just how profound, and (it seems to me) largely unfortunate, Perkins's editorial role had been. For by having the manuscript of *Of Time and the River* changed from first to third person, Wolfe's editor made it appear more, not less, subjective and autobiographical. Told in the first person, the narrative would have had the psychological effect of seeming to be confessional; told in the third person it reads all too much like special pleading—as if Wolfe were hiding behind the pretense that he was writing about a fictional character when in actuality he was writing about himself. Holman has also pointed out, in an as yet unpublished essay, that if the book had been published the way it was written, the long rhetorical pieces and the commentaries would have been grounded in the viewpoint of the first-person narrator, and would thus have much more authority than when simply thrust into a third-person narrative in the form of authorial interjection and rhetorical set-pieces. This is a very good point, it seems to me, though as I have indicated previously, I think that in effect we read *Of Time and the River* in something like that fashion anyway. It is undeniable that in a narrative whose formal dynamics depend upon the relationship between a young autobiographical protagonist and an interpreting authorial spokesman, it would have been far more appropriate and effective to have that relationship recognized and given authority by the clear use of the first person point of view.

In the end, it comes down to the fact that we have still much to learn about Thomas Wolfe. And one reason for the failure of his work to attract definitive criticism, I think, has to do with the problems raised in this essay. Criticism is, after all, an act of the analytical intelligence: and the good literary critic is one who can bring to bear a sophistication of analytical technique that comes of having read, thought about, and understood a considerable range of literature. But since the intense engagement with Thomas Wolfe characteristically occurs when one is first becoming involved with the resources of literature, the chances of it evoking from a critic the kind of critical response that, say, an involvement in the fiction of Faulkner or Joyce or Hemingway can and does sometimes elicit are not especially good.

I seem to be saying in effect that an enthusiasm for Thomas Wolfe goes along with critical immaturity, and that if and when a critic acquires sufficient maturity of taste and judgment, he will know better than to take the fiction of Thomas Wolfe seriously. But that is not it. Good literary criticism is essentially an act of discovery, and the good critic is one who is both equipped and impelled to search out and articulate the nature of his involvement with work that engages his imagination. But since the encounter with Wolfe's fiction comes when it usually does, then by the time the critic possesses the sophistication of technique to deal with what that experience has involved, he will have gone on to other authors and other kinds of literary experience. The critic who, equipped now with the analytical tools for articulating his imaginative engagement with fiction, turns back to look at the Wolfe novels again is characteristically no longer ready for that act of intense personal identification that I have sought to show lies at the heart of the formal dynamics of reading Wolfe. Thus the best writing that has been done about the fiction of Thomas Wolfe, I think, has been written either in affectionate but reluctantly severe memory of a past involvement, or else with a single eye to the defects. This is all right as far as it goes—the defects are abundantly there. But what it has meant is that Wolfe's fiction, by and large, has not received what the work of others of his contemporaries has received: genuinely informed and imaginative critical scrutiny of how it works and why. The corollary to all this, alas, is that much, if not indeed most of the more ambitious and detailed exploration that the Wolfe fiction has elicited has been done uncritically. What C. Hugh Holman declares at the conclusion of his bibliographical essay on scholarship about Thomas Wolfe remains true: "Too much that has been written about Wolfe's work has been called forth as volleys in a heated critical war and too little has been marked by judicious tolerance, good humor, critical acumen, and disinterested seriousness. Wolfe still poses for the critic the persistent questions of autobiography and form, of impassioned rhetoric, and of the present-day validity of the aesthetic assumptions of the nineteenth-century Romantics. His work stands vast, flawed, imperfect, and in its own way magnificent; and it flings down a challege to the serious critic that has largely been ignored." [21]

[21] C. Hugh Holman, "Thomas Wolfe," in Jackson R. Bryer ed., *Fifteen Modern American Authors: A Survey of Research and Criticism* (Durham, N. C.: Duke University Press, 1969), p. 456.

# Thomas Wolfe: Of Time and Neurosis

## by W. M. Frohock

Tom Wolfe's great poem rises out of our national neurosis, and his characteristic anxiety state is one that most of us have experienced in some measure. Much of America is still rural. Most Americans feel that they have rural origins. Yet our centers of education and culture, through which in the process of our growth we naturally pass, are as a rule urban in spirit and sensitive to the metropolitan influence. Thus in the case history of the educated American there is a record of the emotional adjustment by which the two cultures—urban and rural—were more or less successfully brought to terms. The city is always moving ahead and the country always catching up, so that the young man coming out of the country to the city crosses not only a gap of miles but also a gap of years. We live as if in two centuries at once and belong entirely to neither; and the boy who comes from the back-eddy of Maine and arrives on the campus of a New England university wearing his first "College Cut" suit knows as well, by instinct, what Wolfe is talking about as if he had been born in the hills of North Carolina.

Home is the place where you were once and where you really belonged, even though as you remember it you were not always happy there; a part of you which should have been permanent, a place to which you could return after a long stay somewhere else. But it turns out not to be the place where, as Frost says, when you return they have to take you in. It is not in their power to take you in. You have been away, having gone with the premonition that you could not come back, and when you try to return the place has changed and you have changed (O Lost!) and nothing is as it has been. You are, in many senses, the victim of time.

If you are from the South, the feeling may be so much the stronger because you are more aware of the differences. (To find a southerner who is not conscious of being a southerner is rare, whereas your Yankee, for instance, has to migrate from New England to discover that the whole world is not populated by people like himself!) And Wolfe was from North Carolina. Yet the difference was one of degree and not of kind. The breath-taking titles themselves—*Look Homeward, Angel*; *Of Time and the River*; *You Can't Go Home Again*—point to the vast predicament in which a man finds himself trapped and frustrated because everything ebbs, flows, shifts, and refuses to be seen whole; even *The Web and the Rock* juxtaposes an image of permanence with an image of change. And however much his being from the South dramatized this predicament for Wolfe, the predicament is general. It is a paradox that a nation with as short a history as ours should be as obsessed as we are with the flight of time.

Wolfe himself saw the predicament as both general and at the same time extremely personal. The major part of his effort as an artist went into trying to fix the illusory shiftings of memory before they should become lost. Again and again he spoke of his purpose as being to set down, in the time he had, his vision of life. Now, after all the years of controversy since *Look Homeward, Angel* precipitated the sterile debate which centered so often about such questions as whether Wolfe was "magnificently abundant" or "merely garrulous," the scope of his vision remains the central question about him. As he wrote to his old teacher, Mrs. Roberts, he had the Dantesque ambition to create a universe; he did not dodge the question, nor can the serious reader evade it. Every writer of course creates a universe, in the sense, at least, of having to give his characters a world in which to breathe and live. But Wolfe was self-conscious about doing it. He had ready at hand the characters to people his universe. His concern was to give them a habitation, and this habitation is central to his vision.

One might say that he should have written of his ambition to *re*-create a universe. This would have described more accurately the process of recording a vision of the past as viewed through the distorting lens of violent and tortured temperament. "The world I create," he wrote to Mrs. Roberts, ". . . is always inside me." In another connection he wrote that the process of writing a novel was very much as if a great black cloud had gathered inside him and suddenly burst. He never hid—how could he?—the very evident fact that he was writing about himself; the unnecessary little foreword to *Look Homeward, Angel,* in which he defends his method on the somewhat preposterous grounds that there is much of Swift in *Gulliver,* serves only to show how well Wolfe knew what he was doing and how apprehensive he was, as he would always be apprehensive, of what the critics might say. His material was his own experience, as every new fact we learn about him, every new letter published, every anecdote, drives home. Under the name of Eugene Gant or George Webber, the figure of Tom Wolfe always stands in the center of his vision.

How completely different from Dos Passos, who was writing at about the same time and, to a great extent, about the same America! Dos Passos' great strength in *U.S.A.* is his ability to maintain his own detachment. As the result of a discipline which can be traced through his earlier books, Dos Passos can give his reader the feeling that the events which make up his fiction would have taken place just as surely if there had been no novelist at hand to note them down. His ability to establish his perspective—which he finally achieves by the device of presenting his autobiography as a sort of comment on the fiction—has a great deal to do with the success of his great trilogy. Wolfe is the diametrical opposite. The events of his story derive their meaning entirely from their effect upon the central, autobiographical character.

As Dos Passos depends essentially on a discipline which originated in France during the middle years of the nineteenth century, Wolfe seems to go back all the way to the English Romantics. Given the nature of his talent, it is probably just as well that he grew up out of reach of literary modes, that he read more of Virgil than of the little magazines at Asheville, that no one made him give up Melville for Henry James, that he went to the state university and that he reached the literary hotframe of Harvard only after he was a man grown. He seems never to have played the sedulous ape or to have submitted himself to the current literary disciplines or to have acquired the writer's suspicion of himself, of the accuracy of his own senses, or of the validity of his report on them, which marks so much of the literature of our time. He never acquired the constraining awareness of the importance of technique which has conditioned men like Dos Passos. Literary sophistication simply was not his line: who else could have written, with anything like Wolfe's unawareness of the ludicrous side of what he was doing, his endless variations on lines from Shakespeare? One of his major sources of strength was that he was so completely and miraculously out of date. "I began life," he wrote, again to Mrs. Roberts, "as a lyric writer." He ended life as nothing else.

Romantic lyric poetry—and we are agreed that Wolfe's poem is romantic in many ways, including the way of revolt—is the poetry of youth. The greatest praise we give to a poet who in mature years writes lyrics of freshness and originality is that he "seems so young." This strikes me as one of the most helpful keys to Wolfe; his vision of life and the world in which he makes his characters live are the vision and the world of a very young man.

He felt himself so wretchedly, so miserably and so magnificently alone. Despite all his use of the second person plural, Eugene Gant and George Webber never escape the feeling that their enterprises are personal and special, their cases unique. There is a story about Wolfe, that once when he was riding downtown after a baseball game he suddenly alarmed a subway car by screaming, "The bastards are ambushing me!" According to this story—which for all I know is apocryphal—Wolfe had been talking to a friend about literary critics, but the world's series crowd on the subway did not know this, did not know Wolfe and probably had not read his books, so that his outburst occasioned no little surprise. Now no one who has read his Wolfe faithfully would, or should, have been surprised in the least. The point is that we were all bastards—there was Tom Wolfe and then there were all the other people who were not Tom Wolfe and they were aliens. He went alone.

If his great feeling of loneliness was not pathological, it was at least exaggerated. He hated many things because they were not himself: Negroes (much of the time) and Irish Catholics (or at least the Boston Irish) and Brahmins and Jews. Eugene Gant and

George Webber are repelled, immediately or eventually, by most of the people with whom they come in contact. The record of the autobiographical character's inability to establish satisfactory communication with other human beings suggests a fundamental difficulty, a failure to understand and to be understood, which may in turn be related to the state of compulsive frenzy in which Wolfe appears to have done much of his writing. With Wolfe, as with Céline, the other novelist of our time who approaches Wolfe in this matter of being repelled by people, one cannot help feeling that the drive to write, and to keep on writing at whatever cost in prolixity and reiteration, is tied up with some sort of despair of ever being fully understood.

Yet the exaggeration, painful as its results may be at times both to Wolfe and his reader, seems only the magnification of one aspect of the time-neurosis which so generally affects Wolfe's vision and which indeed afflicts so many of the rest of us. We live, by circumstances of our birth and culture, in two periods at once and are completely at home in neither. If we do not, as Eugene Gant did, envy the English family which appears in *Of Time and the River* simply because for all their stuffiness they were so thoroughly at home where they were, or if we do not envy a man like Morison who is so sure of being understood that he converses always in ejaculations and fragments of sentences, the hero's underlying feeling of isolation, which makes him envy them, is certainly not foreign to us: transplantation implies that for a long time the plant will not take root firmly. Wolfe comes by the feeling of isolation very honestly indeed.

We have come, of late, to feel that the presence of this theme of isolation makes the mood of a novel tragic. In Wolfe's case, however, it seems clear that the exaggerated feeling of man's loneliness which permeates his work, and which conditions his whole somewhat neurotic vision of life, prevents that vision from being a truly tragic one. At this point, a comparison with the work of André Malraux becomes almost inevitable.

Wolfe and Malraux, better than any other contemporaries who come to mind, have caught up and made their own the feeling of man's solitude. Malraux's early jungle tale, *The Royal Way*, is full of this great loneliness which is accompanied, as it is also in Wolfe, by an almost overwhelming awareness of the imminence of death. In Malraux's other novels (*The Conquerors, Man's Fate*) the principal characters are beset by the problem of breaking through this lone-liness into a feeling of community with their fellows. In the act of killing by stealth, Tchen, in *Man's Fate,* is somewhat less bothered by the fact of murder than by the solitude which terrifies him as he commits it. Most of the other characters in the book experience something similar. But certain of them, at least, overcome this feel-ing of isolation. They go down, but they go in the knowledge that their fate is *man's* fate. And this is precisely the book which made European critics so aware of the possibilities of the tragic novel. Malraux proceeded, in *Days of Wrath,* to write a novel—little known in America—which in its mood, its highly compact and concentrated form, its insistence on struggle, its atmosphere of vio-lence, comes as near to being pure tragedy, I believe, as a novel can come. This is the story of a man imprisoned by the Nazis, whose strength to undergo imprisonment and torture and finally to escape comes from his discovering that even in the solitude of a Nazi prison no man is ever completely alone. In a preface to the book, Malraux insists that man's loneliness and man's essential solidarity are equally important; they may not be separated.

Malraux's mature awareness of the two faces to the medal is what Wolfe seems to me never to have attained. He never convinced himself that no man is an island. Wolfe's feeling of solitude—to-gether with his awareness of the erosions of time and the imminent presence of death—appears, in comparison with Malraux's later work, as a badge of immaturity. Not that this condemns him; many writers as great as and greater than Wolfe have been immature in this sense. But their achievement has nothing to do with tragedy; and neither has his. The feeling of loneliness, and of the individ-ual's being so bafflingly penned within himself, prevents it. The first person singular, as has often been remarked, is not the appro-priate pronoun for tragedy.

It would be pointless, of course, to worry such a question unless in the process we got a fresh view of what Wolfe was and of what he did. It is very likely that his chronic immaturity—moral and aesthetic—warped his vision of life.

For all the lore about Wolfe—and many strange yarns are abroad about him—we really know little about him as a private person. Most of his published letters have been literary and, in a way, formal. The Wolfe legend is doubtless as undependable as it is picturesque; he probably was never so colossally incapable of telling the unembellished truth about himself as many stories (such as the one about his persistent complaint that he was starving like Chatterton in a garret, when actually he lived where he did only from inertia) made him seem. In his books he sounds like one of the people—Stendhal was another—who spend their lives trying to see themselves as they are without ever quite penetrating the thick wall of self-delusion.

His ability to make incredible things seem credible is itself almost incredible. It is only when one goes back to *Look Homeward, Angel* that the Aeschylean family of the early book shows itself for what it is and the whole Pentland-Gant clan becomes implausible if not preposterous. W. O. Gant as Agamemnon home from the wars to die, Eliza as Clytemnestra (her refusal to admit that there is anything wrong with the old man being a kind of murder), Helen as Electra when she is not doubling as Cassandra, Eugene as the wretched Orestes . . . one feels that Wolfe cannot really have intended these things, and yet, vaguely, there they are! The people, if hardly the setting, of an *Oresteia*. The family taint on which Eliza and Helen dwell is the Curse upon the House. And on first reading, or if one has read *Look Homeward, Angel* and no more, one accepts these things unthinkingly; the Gant-Pentland tribe seems plausible indeed when taken by itself.

But when one gets out of Altamont into the wider world of *Of Time and the River,* he begins to see that too many people are like the Gants and the Pentlands; there are simply too many queer ducks. Robert Weaver, drinking himself to pieces and already showing marks of the insanity "that will destroy him"; Francis Starwick, prey of a diabolical absence of passion; George Thornton, in the quiet depths of whose eyes "the fatal madness which would destroy him was already legible"; Bascom Pentland, the crazy uncle in Boston married to the crazy wife; the inordinately vulgar John T. Brill—with such people around it is impossible not to feel that we have strayed into some gallery of eccentrics. At times it seems as if everyone Wolfe writes about is abnormal, or else downright

insane. And after we have seen these people we look back at Altamont and are much less impressed by the extraordinary population
of *Look Homeward, Angel*; the Aeschylean family now appear as
only the first in a long succession of crackpot figures. There is small
doubt that something in Wolfe's vision has warped them. All of
them are a little like the policemen who pick up Eugene and his
friends for drunken driving in a little South Carolina town.

> And these huge creatures evoked for Eugene a whole history of this
> earth and people, monstrous, savage, and unutterable—a congruent
> and unspeakable legend which he knew, and all of them knew, down
> to the roots, and which he could not speak about and had to speak
> about, somehow, or die. For in these men there was evident not only
> the savage and mindless energy of the earth itself, with all that was
> wild, sensual, fecund, cruel and good-natured—the whole weather of
> life—but there was also evident the fear, the shame, the horror that
> had crushed them beneath its ocean weight of nameless and cowering
> dread, and broken or destroyed their souls.

Applied to a squad of country cops, this is evidently and clum-
sily out of proportion, but the fact is that Wolfe saw most of his
characters in some such light. And because of this extravagance
which works to prevent the appearance of any group of reasonably
life-size characters in his books by which to measure the outsize of
the others, those others, the important ones, lose something of their
stature, even in *Look Homeward, Angel* and *You Can't Go Home
Again.*

I had better open an apologetic parenthesis here to explain that,
to my taste, *Look Homeward, Angel* and *You Can't Go Home
Again* are by far the best parts of Wolfe's long novel. In spite of
what I have been saying about them, these two books, describing
the preparation of Eugene's departure, and the later discovery that,
as he had suspected before leaving, true return was impossible,
haunt me as no other books written in America have ever done.
But the other two, the story of what happened to Gant-Webber
between the departure and the attempted return, seem to me less
important. Possibly this is because what happens in the first and
last books of the series is what happens, in some degree, to every
American, whereas what happens in the middle volumes is more
special; much that occurs in *The Web and the Rock* could happen

only to a rising American novelist. Possibly there is another reason: it is also true that *Look Homeward, Angel* was the work of an unknown on whom the editor could exert the authority of experience, and *You Can't Go Home Again* was edited after Wolfe's death left the editor with a relatively free hand, whereas the middle volumes were products of years when Wolfe had become extremely sensitive on the subject of editing. But whatever the reason, the second and third books are spotty. Pick up any copy of *Of Time and the River* and hold the page-edges to the light; the darkened sections are sure signs that the book has been read as if it were an anthology. After the first time, one does not voluntarily read his way through the 900-odd pages of this book again. One goes directly to certain parts—some of the best writing Wolfe ever did—like the death of Eugene's father, the race between the trains, the station stop in Troy, the visit to Joel Pierce's icebox. As novels, that is to say *as wholes,* the middle books do not seem to me to stand with the other two.

Reading *Of Time and the River* directly after *Look Homeward, Angel* throws a revealing light on the people of the latter book. The Gants and Pentlands become not tragic but queer; not people working out their destiny, but frustrate victims of time. Their violence, instead of being the inevitable result of forces which drive them in a given direction, is merely the inevitable result of frazzled nerves. A typical case of this, perhaps the most eloquent that Wolfe ever invented, is a struggle between Eugene and his brother Luke, which takes place in their mother's living room. There is no point to the fight, nothing is at stake; doing physical damage to each other will accomplish no more than the temporary relief of the exasperation. This is violence without significance. Compare it with the fighting in *The Grapes of Wrath* or with the last chapter of *For Whom the Bell Tolls* and the distinction is clear. These are eccentrics clawing at each other; they are frustrated even in the attempt to do lasting harm; and this is the best proof possible that the people Wolfe sees, as he sees them, are not tragic figures.

Straightway we also doubt the reality of the places where Wolfe makes them move. Originally we accepted Altamont without question, but just as we suspect that the people are distorted as soon as we leave Altamont for Cambridge, so we also suspect Altamont itself as soon as we can put it in the new perspective. Wolfe's New England makes Altamont a never-never land.

> . . . New England, with its harsh and stony soil, and its tragic and lonely beauty; its desolate rocky coasts and its swarming fisheries, the white, piled, frozen bleakness of its winters with the magnificent jewelry of stars, the dark firwoods, and the warm little white houses at which it is impossible to look without thinking of groaning bins, hung bacon, hard cider, succulent bastings and love's warm, white, and opulent flesh.

Harsh New England certainly is and there is no exaggerating the stoniness of its soil. Its beauty is lonely and can be tragic if you want it to be. And so forth. But New England is above all the homeland of shortage and worry, of industries that move out and of young people who emigrate because New England cannot support the children it spawns, and of old people who stay on to grub what living they can from the farms and—along the main roads—from the tourists. There is indeed a school of New England romanticists who write stuff of the "succulent bastings" sort, and there are apparently readers for it, but the difference between Wolfe's New England and the New England of people like Professor Robert P. T. Coffin is that Wolfe seems actually to believe that his New England exists. It doesn't. Here where the wind is always north-northeast, as Robinson says, care is the rule—not plenty and not sensuousness. Those cozy little white houses have but one warm room in them during the winter and upstairs the chamber-pots are frozen before morning; the succulent bastings are in the writer's mind; and love's flesh is rough with goose-pimples.

Wolfe's New York is probably better. New York is at least so various that nothing said of it can be convicted of falsehood. But here again, as Wolfe watches the gray-faced, hostile millions stream through the subways, he is an outsider. There is always something about him that suggests that he is again looking in at the cozy little white houses. The intimate sentiment of New York, which Dos Passos has in spite of all the Sandburg-Millay romanticism of the big city permeating *Manhattan Transfer,* is not in Wolfe.

It is in the nature of his talent that he should see things from the outside only, and be forced always to guess what is inside them;

his vision is the vision of the outsider; and this again is a part of the national neurosis out of which, I am arguing, his vision rises and which warps it. Thus the question naturally arises, after we have finished looking at his middle books, whether his view of Altamont is not the vision of an outsider also. Did this youth of sixteen ever read all the books Wolfe talks about, or are these the reading experiences of a mature man, garnered at the University of North Carolina and at Harvard and thrown back in memory to be associated with the wrong age? And did the still younger lad, delivering papers in Altamont's Niggertown, experience all its alien mystery then, or are these also the emotions of a later age thrown back upon adolescence? All these things in *Look Homeward, Angel* sound much more like a relatively older person, deep in his first work at the age of twenty-four, when he has left Altamont far behind him— as if they were a confused reconstruction of memories. No growing youth was ever quite so full of literature, never felt anything with quite such transcendent keenness, any more than the Gant-Pentland family was ever quite so monstrous as Wolfe makes it look. The reconstruction of the past is a notoriously tricky enterprise and Wolfe has been tricked in it.

Thus, to the earlier remark that the first person singular is not the appropriate pronoun for tragedy, we must add that the perfect is not the appropriate tense. Recollection of tragic events does not make tragedy. To get the full force of the tragic situation we need to feel contemporaneous with it; the author has to show the action as it takes place, not as it is rebuilt in retrospect. And so Wolfe's novels are not tragic, not only because they are so exclusively personal but because his attitude toward his material, with special respect to time, is not a tragic attitude. It is dominantly emotion recollected.

But not emotion recollected in tranquillity. Wolfe's poetry is not calmly and quietly intense; his main theme is the theme of being lost in America, and it is treated by a poet who is still lost. His perspective of America itself is out of joint: distances and spaces are magnified, a trip from New York to North Carolina becomes a journey "down the continent"; much of his America is an abstraction. He has some of the naturalistic pantheism, the feeling that man and the soil are intimately bound together in essence, which marks so much Western literature since Zola and which makes him sound occasionally like Jean Giono, just as he shows at times some of the enthusiasm for being American, if not for the faith democratic, of Walt Whitman. Now and again he reveals a feeling for, though not much knowledge of, the history of our people—the feeling that this land is something apart because the dust of his ancestors is mixed with its dust. But mostly his complaint is that these things do not mean more to him than they do, that he really has no place and "no door where he can enter," and that meanwhile he is being swept along by the stream of time. The answer to his eternal question is not the answer of Whitman and Crane and Paul Engle. The one thing that he can be sure of, the one door that must open for him, is death.

Wolfe is the writer of our century who has written most eloquently about death—the death of Grover, the death of Ben, of old Gant; and of the overwhelming imminence of death everywhere. As each individual submerges beneath the river of time, something of Wolfe himself is lost, each was a parcel of his consciousness. More surely than anything else the thought of death looses that remarkable flow of his language—the unearthly torrent of words which has always been the delight of some of his critics and the bane of the rest—and also the extraordinary resources of his rhetoric.

The rhetoric is essential. One reads much more about Wolfe's breadth of vocabulary and his obviously sensuous pleasure in words, and of what someone has called his multitudinous garrulity, than about the way he used his gift. He has the distinction of being the one writer of his generation who truly dared pull out all the stops. Dos Passos cannot compete with him in this respect, because Dos Passos' method of seeing and recording impressions calls for finding the perfectly right word, and the perfectly right word is obscured if associated with a half-dozen approximately right words; and besides, the completely successful word for Dos Passos needs the least possible rhetorical support: where each word stands completely for an impression the only real linkage needed is that of consciousness, proximity to the word which denotes the preceding impression in the series. Hemingway cannot compete because his instinctive emotional key, subdued and uneloquent, will not permit, and because his favorite characters are frequently talkative but rarely eloquent people.

Wolfe and his characters, on the other hand, have the native eloquence of an old-time political orator. He needs every resource of rhetorical structure to support the great weight of his enormous enumerations, which are as heavy as Dreiser's. It is extraordinary how often the rhetoric of his own sentences is identical with the drunken rhetoric which he puts in the sonorous mouth of the old man Gant, the great difference of course being that Gant has the rhetorical structure he needs, but not the words to go with it; whereas Wolfe has the words.

> The hands had given to the interminable protraction of his living death a kind of concrete horror that it otherwise would not have had. For as his powerful gaunt figure waned and wasted under the ravages of the cancer that was consuming him until he had become only the enfeebled shadow of his former self, his gaunt hands, on which there was so little which death could consume, lost none of their former rock-like heaviness, strength and shapely power. Thus, even when the giant figure of the man had become nothing but a spectral remnant of itself, sunk in a sorrow of time, awaiting death, those great, still-living hands of power and strength hung incredibly, horribly, from that spectral form of death to which they were attached.

The words are here. And so also are most of the faults against which the manuals of English continually warn: prolixity, punning, cliché, repetitiousness and the rest. What saves it? It seems to me that in passages like this Wolfe skates determinedly around the edges of the hackneyed, rescuing himself each time through the presence of the particular word which redeems the rest and keeps the phrase from being irremediable cliché: in the first sentence "interminable protraction" saves the hackneyed "living death"; in the second, the appearance of the verb "waned"—entirely unexpected and acquiring from its context a meaning it never quite had before—stands in relation to the other verb, "wasted," as "enfeebled" stands to the rest of what would otherwise be the deadly cliché, "shadow of his former self." Such rhetorical repetitions as "spectral remnant," which picks up the earlier "shadow," and "spectral form" which in turn picks up "spectral remnant," are the sources of a freshness which is all the more perceptible because on analysis we are convinced that it comes from reviving what, except in the hands of Thomas Wolfe, would be entirely beyond hope of resuscitation.

All of this is related to Wolfe's habit of taking up some of the most familiar lines of the literary heritage and making them new and strange by the changing of a word or so: "It was unbelievable that an old cancer-riddled spectre of a man should have so much blood in him." I can remember offhand three separate places where he plays variations on the old man with so much blood in him. Despite our awareness that Wolfe abuses this device—as for that matter he abuses, sooner or later, most other rhetorical devices—its value to him is palpable. The essence of this we find in Shakespeare himself, in such lines as

> . . . the feet
> That fourteen hundred years ago were nailed
> For our advantage to the bitter cross

wherein a word like "bitter," common as dirt itself, of its own strength lifts an ordinary prose discourse into poetry. Wolfe's gift is of the same kind. The result is the sort of boldness which allows him to get away with the obvious—note the repeated pun on Gant's name in the passage above, and the association of "rock-like heaviness" with the hands of a man who has always been a stonecutter. This is the kind of eloquence that Wolfe brings to the themes of time and of death, time's child.

It is impossible to read Wolfe and like him without becoming something of an anthologist. And since each reader of Wolfe has his own favorite selections, I am offering here at least one example of his poetry of time:

> . . . it is not the slow, the punctual sanded drip of the unnumbered days that we remember best, the ash of time; nor is it the huge monotone of the lost years, the unswerving schedules of the lost life and the well-known faces, that we remember best . . .

This is the poetry of a theme on which John Dos Passos, with a poet's discipline turned to his special uses, was writing the prose.

There is no point in denying that often Wolfe let go to print much that should never have gone. Those of us who like him believe that there was a god in him, but a very unruly god who gave him no peace and at times went away without warning, as people sometimes go away and leave a radio with the switch turned on playing in an empty tenement. He was an enthusiast who had, as old Gant had, "a tragic consciousness of time," and of death. Like the people in *Look Homeward, Angel* he was a fanatic, and time and death were his obsessions. Consequently, in those moments when the god is absent he sounds like a hysterical woman who insists on feeling unloved, while life slips away without anything really stable appearing amid the flow of existence—a hysterical woman whose life is a great conspiracy to frustrate her.

Much that he wrote proves that the critics who were hell-bent to show what really needed no demonstration, i.e., that he did not know how to compose, were right, and is evidence of the compulsive frenzy in which he wrote. It was often more important to him to finish saying something and get on to saying something else, than to take care for the nicety of the saying. Edward Aswell has done his best to dispel the legend that Wolfe never rewrote, and other critics who have examined Wolfe's style closely have found a change appearing in the later work; but there remains abundant proof he did not rewrite enough. Words obsess him, and rhetoric sweeps him away. Such things as Francis Starwick's having a "rather womanish" voice almost *ad infinitum,* the appearance of words like "octopal" in and out of acceptable context on so many occasions, the inability to stop ringing the changes on lines like the one about the old man with all the blood in him, the multiple repetitions of such an intuition as that Uncle Bascom's head is like Emerson's— and so on indefinitely—simply mar his work. They also testify to the great truth of Wolfe's own remark that at times when he wrote it felt as if a great black cloud had discharged itself inside him. Wolfe knew his weakness; he was haunted by the example of Flaubert, and grateful to Maxwell Perkins for assuring him that it was not necessary to be "the Flaubert kind of writer." He finally changed from Scribner to Harper in order to prove to his detractors that he, and not Maxwell Perkins, was the one who put the books together. Our criticism of him will become more cogent as we give over arguing about this incontrovertible weakness and go on to define, as precisely as we can, Wolfe's great strength.

A long time ago the French philosopher Diderot, busy with a discussion on institutions among the savages of the South Seas, paused a moment to remark how contrary to common sense it seems, in a world where time is always at work and change is the rule, to base marriage on the assumption that love is eternal. Years later his countryman, Musset, picked up the theme in a famous poem, *Le Souvenir,* in which he added a new ingredient: how sad and how poignant that the eternity of the love we swear is, of necessity, an illusion. The difference between the two points of view is probably the essential difference between the eighteenth century and the nineteenth; Diderot's reflection was prompted merely by the fact that he was having a certain amount of trouble with his wife —a situation which he managed somehow to take pretty much in stride—whereas Musset, frustrated in his various attempts to realize a completely satisfactory love, generalizes his predicament into an essential aspect of man's fate. This mood is Wolfe's, leaving out love or substituting for it the whole complex of man's emotions. It puts him in the tradition of Proust . . . and of Dos Passos, a very central and important tradition since it reflects in literature the great discovery of the relativity of all things which is our inheritance from the nineteenth century. But the tradition itself does not need to be eternal, and the feeling we have that after Proust and Dos Passos and Wolfe there was left, *circa* 1930, very little to be said about it, is probably the best indication we have that by that date the nineteenth century was over.

# The Rhetoric and the Agony

## by *Alfred Kazin*

At twenty-two, when he was studying dramaturgy under Professor Baker at Harvard, Wolfe wrote to his mother:

> I know this now: I am inevitable, I sincerely believe. The only thing that can stop me now is insanity, disease, or death. . . . [Life] is not all bad, but it is not all good; it is not all ugly, but it is not all beautiful; it is life, life, life—the only thing that matters. It is savage, cruel, kind, noble, passionate, generous, stupid, ugly, beautiful, painful, joyous—it is all these and more—and it's all these I want to know, and BY GOD I shall, though they crucify me for it. I will go to the end of the earth to find it, to understand it. I will know this country when I am through as I know the palm of my hand, and I will put it on paper and make it true and beautiful.

When he died in September, 1938, not yet thirty-eight, he was what the world calls a leading novelist; but no one would have called him a prodigy. There have been writers, like the twenty-five-year-old Keats whose last letters are moving in their very profundity, who compressed all maturity into their boyhood, and even transcended it. Wolfe was always a boy, a very remarkable boy; and his significance as a writer is that he expanded his boyhood into a lifetime, made it exciting and important, even illuminated many of the problems that give life its common savor, without ever transcending the alienation and pain of his boyhood. "All this hideous doubt, despair, and dark confusion of the soul a lonely man must know, for he is united to no image save that which he creates himself," he wrote in "God's Lonely Man," a frankly autobiographical essay which he composed and recomposed many times; "he is bolstered by no other knowledge save that which he can gather for himself with the vision of his own eyes and brain." This feverish dependence upon himself, a fantastically uninhibited innocence, was his torment and his advantage. Naïve, self-absorbed, full of homespun mysticism and adolescent grandeur, he cut his way blindly and noisily to achievement; by his passionate insistence on the importance of self, that self is the very center of existence, he gave his fever and uncertainty a remarkable scope and something more than the dignity of the conventionally mature understanding. Believing in nothing but his own power, he infected the world of his novels with it. He made his characters larger than life without suggesting that they were superior to, or removed from, it. He lived in a world in which man was forever haunted by his own promise and deflected from it. Inevitably, there were no half-tones in that world, as there were few gradations and nuances in Wolfe's own mind; man lived by compromises with fate, or conquered (as perhaps only the artist spirit could conquer) by a supreme contempt for it. Believing so completely in the possibility of happiness, he gave human ambition, human valor, human expression, a rooted strength in nature, the quality of primeval fact.

"I believe that we are lost here in America, but I believe we shall be found," Wolfe wrote in his last letter to "Foxhall Edwards" in *You Can't Go Home Again*. ". . . I think that the true discovery of America is before us. I think the true fulfillment of our spirit, of our people, of our mighty and immortal land, is yet to come." Seemingly, then, it was not only life as an idea, but life as victory, that possessed him; the very callowness of his more expansive flights persuades one of that. In a world of endless possibilities and limitless power—that is, a world seen refracted through such a mind as Wolfe's—every object, properly understood, possessed an incredible radiance, and every function had its heroic purpose. He wrote one book all his life, as all the volumes he produced were chapters in it; and his hero—now Eugene Gant, now George Webber, now Orestes, now Faust, now Telemachus in search of the father and Proteus in the sea world of the city, now Jason on the eternal voyage and Antaeus back to earth, now Kronos dreaming of time and Faust gazing at Helen—was able to bestride cities, to hear in every love urge the detonations of "fate," to feel every twinge as a blow, every yawn as a snicker, to hear as from his own heart the music of multitudes, to read a hundred books and guess at the contents of a thousand, to eat like a regiment, to bellow at the universe and hear it whimper submissively back.

That persistent yearning, that ambiguous universal victory, is Wolfe's most palpable memorial, the testimony he gave to the world in a raging torrent of words, the thing he wished most to believe true of himself. And it was, in a sense, the real Wolfe, as every facet of his mind and impulse of his tumultuous consciousness represented the "real" Wolfe. Yet it is impossible to appreciate his achievement, as it is impossible to understand what constituted his literary mind and character, if one misses the extraordinary deliberateness of his total conception, and the self-consciousness (in the best sense a self-understanding) of his life and purpose. For to an extent that seems almost unreal Wolfe did embody the conflict between the modern individual and society; he even found his central theme in that conflict, where so many different and certainly more interesting talents have merely moved in its atmosphere. The feverishness and wayward exultation of his novels mark only one aspect of that conflict, for he had a keen, if seemingly eccentric, social intelligence, an insight into the pattern of events and societies seemingly beyond him, that became part of his subject as much as his rhetoric supported it. He was not a novelist *of* society; he was a refraction of everything in society that he saw in some vital relation to his own individuality. Yet his native innocence and romantic self-trust were such that his mimicry (much of Wolfe's "objective" realism is strained, if powerfully successful, mimicry) attained the level of satire and a sweeping symbolic tragedy. "His aim," as John Peale Bishop has written, "was to set down America as far as it can belong to the experience of one man." In no other writer in America after Whitman could that aim have been realized; in no other, not even Whitman, was the sense of that need so apparently voracious and insistent.

Describing "Eugene Gant" at twelve, Wolfe wrote in *Look Homeward, Angel*: "He had learned by now to project himself mechanically before the world, an acceptable counterfeit of himself which would protect him from intrusion." From the very first the long epic

of self to which he devoted his life became the history of his tribu-
lations, a history of his self's struggle against all the manifold
threats, humiliations, paralyzing cautions and frustrations, which
composed his outer experience—the enemy which he had to destroy
in order to conquer—that is, to live truly, at all. The theme, then,
was the conflict between the "I" and the world, that first person in
which he began to write *Look Homeward, Angel,* and which slipped,
like a Freudian gamin, through the rough disguise of Eugene Gant
in *Of Time and the River.* In his first novel the enemy was the
world narrowed to the first horizon of a child's sensations, and
found its abundant representation in his mother Eliza, her greed
and lovelessness and talk, the burning acquisitiveness which found
its symbol in the boardinghouse that supplanted their home, the
family's slow disintegration, his newspaper route in the early winter
mornings—a mother in whom he recognized a fateful source of his
torment, as he saw its theatrical reflection in his father. And struggling against his mother and the experience she at once represented
and imposed upon him, Wolfe was struggling with even more painful ardor and bewilderment against those in his own family—Ben
and Helen particularly—who had submitted and been defeated. Or,
in making his newspaper rounds in the Negro quarters, he was re-
belling simultaneously against the hysterical "success" of his brother
Luke, the frenzied Oliver Optic mind stammering its way to the
forlorn middle-class victory of money and status.

"Lost, lost, forever lost," he wrote of his kind in the anguished
little prose lyric that became the leit-motif of his work. *"Naked and
alone we came into exile. In her dark womb we did not know our
mother's face; from the prison of her flesh have we come into the
unspeakable and incommunicable prison of this earth."* Doomed as
they all were, they represented even more the threat of his own
doom, the enemy made symbol, the symbol made flesh. Even the
very young Eugene, describing himself as a child at the fair, became
the Romantic Self. "His mind, just emerging from the unreal wilderness of childish fancy, gave way completely in this Fair, and he
was paralyzed by the conviction, which often returned to him in
later years, that his life was a fabulous nightmare and that, by
cunning and conspirate artifice, he had surrendered all his hope,
belief, and confidence to the lewd torture of demons masked in

human flesh." In the light of that conviction, so remarkably un-
changed to the end as to seem the very principle of Wolfe's existence, his every experience became an encounter with the Enemy,
a measure of defeat or apotheosis. With the same ingenuous grandeur with which he wrote the story of his trip from Asheville to
Harvard on a scale larger than that which Homer had permitted
himself in the *Odyssey*, Wolfe went on to describe the enemy in all
its subsequent manifestations—Harvard and "The School for Utility
Cultures" in New York, the "Rock City" and the Jews; the Hudson
River gentry and Brooklyn and the New York intellectuals; Esther
Jack, the Jewish mistress who became associated in his mind with
all that was opulent and proud and corrupt in the metropolitan
culture; his old neighbors and relatives and friends in "Altamont"
and "Libya Hill," who had read their own portraits in his first book,
and hated him for it.

In this struggle between two absolutes, the "I" and the Enemy
world, Wolfe found the theme of his rhetoric, and the source of the
imagery—swollen and turgid, yet curiously dramatic—that illuminated the struggle in his own mind and sustained it by symbols. The
prime symbol, always, was the image of the Father, the gate that
would open the doors of the prison house for him. "The deepest
search in life, it seemed to me, the thing that in one way or another was central to all living," he wrote in *The Story of a Novel*,
"was man's search for a father, not merely the father of his flesh,
not merely the lost father of his youth, but the image of a strength
and wisdom external to his need and superior to his hunger, to
which the belief and power of his own life could be united." The
image of the Gate that recurred in his works (*"Where shall the
weary rest? When shall the lonely of heart come home? What doors
are open for the wanderer? And which of us shall find his father,
know his face, and in what place, and in what time, and in what
land? Where?"*) thus became the theme of his pilgrimage, the gate-
way to reality and happiness. But with it was united in Wolfe's
mind the sense that this was somehow related to the American loneliness, the perpetual American migration, the loneliness of the artist-
spirit in America that could so easily become the loneliness of all
its young men and ardent spirits. Lost, lost, forever lost. "We are
so lost, so naked and so lonely in America," he wrote over and

again. "Immense and cruel skies bend over us, and all of us are driven on forever and we have no home." The Romantic "I" he remained to the end, consciously writing the story of his life and of all existence within the framework of that personal epic struggle; but the "I" became more than Thomas Eugene Gant Wolfe, or Thomas George Webber Wolfe. It became (with the same facile incandescence with which Whitman had associated himself with the hero of *Leaves of Grass,* and *Leaves of Grass* with all America) the moral history of the Young American, even of modern American life. For the second of his primal symbols was the Rock, the city world and the city darkness, the flowing river of time that absorbed and dissipated life; and as the Father image represented the yearning for freedom, and the Rock the waste and chagrin of experience, so only the artist's "I" could mediate between them and conquer the Enemy.

In this light Wolfe's perpetual recourse to America as an idea, the seeming paradox between his frenzied self-interest and his assumption of a moral authority in which he spoke for all the lost young men in America, even for all America itself, was not a paradox or a sentimentally expansive gesture at all, but the necessary consequence of his situation and his understanding. For though he used his life and art interchangeably in this quest (so that the relations between them were perhaps as dark and radiantly confused as they are to us), they were, taken together, a reflection of Wolfe's conviction that he himself was a prime symbol of American experience and of a perpetual American ambition. In his quest for grandeur, his very thinking in terms of grandeur, his self-trust and self-absorption announced that he had found America in himself, and that if he was alone in America, America was alone among the nations of the world, and incomparable in its range and fervor, its spiritual quality and aspiration. Hence the further significance of his need to set all of America down on paper, as Whitman had done. Hence his recurrent effort (always using his life and art interchangeably, always using his life not as the material of art but as the very voice of his art) to capture America as an idea and to master it as one, since in his own mind he was a spiritual agent, speaking and acting for others, and always in the name of nationality and destiny.

It was in this spirit, certainly, that Wolfe sought to make monuments, to "set down America as far as it can belong to the experience of one man." He was not "celebrating" America, as Whitman had done; he was trying to record it, to assimilate it, to echo it in himself. This, the very quality and turn of his abundant energy, was the source of his frenzied passion for American details, of his need to reproduce them exactly for the substance of his art. Sitting in a Paris café, he would remember the railing on the Atlantic City boardwalk, an iron bridge across an American river, the clink of a milkman's horse going slowly up the morning street. He set down with agonizing precision the look on the face of an old teacher, the mountain coldness and Appalachian heights back home, the tone of boys playing one-o'-cat in the sleepy twilight. In *You Can't Go Home Again* he wrote of George Webber:

> He spent weeks and months trying to put down on paper the exactitudes of countless fragments—what he called "the dry, caked colors of America"—how the entrance to a subway looked, the design and webbing of the elevated structure, the look and feel of an iron rail, the particular shade of rusty green with which so many things are painted in America. Then he tried to pin down the foggy color of the brick of which so much of London is constructed, the look of an English doorway, of a French window, of the roofs and chimney pots of Paris, of a whole street in Munich—and each of these foreign things he then examined in contrast to its American equivalent.

This passion for accumulation was not, however, a sentimental habit or even the mere reflex of his energy. He was offering America, or the possible idea of America, as a standard and as a reaction against all the sloth, degeneration, weakness, and cynicism which he saw in that Enemy which had become the symbol of everything he hated and feared. It is precisely because he was not merely "celebrating" America, in Whitman's sense, that he thought of his own struggle and of the necessary moral struggle in contemporary life in the same terms. Believing rapturously in the Romantic "I," he extended that faith, as he extended almost everything else, into a counterpoise to chaos. As Whitman had come at the beginning, when America was shapeless and nascent, so Wolfe thought of himself as coming at the climacteric, when the choice between the promise and its disillusionment, between life and death even, summoned all a man's resources—his own resources above all. From one point of view, of course, this was the most monstrous of his confusions, for he was not thinking, like Whitman, of a new conception in terms of a new subject ("the Promise of These States"). He was not, that is to say, a moral intelligence working itself out exhilaratingly and indiscriminately, a powerful romantic spirit who caught fire from every phase of contemporary experience, an antebellum Everyman who had absorbed his own personality in his countrymen and found his values in their celebration. Where Whitman had identified himself with his America out of a supreme act of fellowship, the radiant confidence possible only to him and his time, Wolfe made his self equal to the communal tragedy he saw and wished to describe; he kept to the "I" as Whitman never did. This, perhaps, is the larger significance of his inveterate self-interest, and the reason why he became the least interestitng character in his work, and certainly the character in all his books one knows least. He could prove himself a striking realist of contemporary society, but at bottom his sense of tragedy was always a personal complaint, an imperial maladjustment. For if he knew the significance behind "the malady of the ideal," knew it with an excruciating pain and intensity and livid precision unmatched by his contemporaries, it was always, at bottom, because his experience was what sustained and afflicted *him;* it was because he wanted, consciously and dynamically, more of America than it was prepared to give him. He thought of himself as writing the last great epic of American nationality, certainly the last great American romance, as perhaps he did; but the epic was a personal quarrel, and the romance a vast inchoate yearning to the end.

That Wolfe proved himself the most self-centered and most inclusive novelist of the day is thus no paradox. His imagination was a perpetual tension between his devotion to himself and his devotion to his self's interests and symbolism, and he made his art out of the equation he drew. It is this that explains why Wolfe, in no real sense an objective novelist, was yet one who incorporated the best methods of American realism and passed beyond them; and it is this that explains why, though he often seemed determined to prove himself the sickliest of romantic egotists, he was, ironically enough, the most alert and brilliant novelist of depression America, and an extraordinarily imaginative analyst of American types and the social disorganization of the thirties. Though the feverish surface of his work hardly suggests it, he did write on several levels. Just as his imagination had presented his own situation and the American situation as coeval, so he was not always the stricken child wailing through thousands of pages of epic unhappiness—lost, lost, forever lost—but a prophetic voice who brought the same shattering intensity to his studies of contemporary demoralization, the climate of Fascism in Europe and America, the confusion and rout of the masses, that he did to his self-torment and yearning for personal freedom and redemption; brought it, indeed, with a conviction of absolute harrowing need and sense of achievement that made him seem the richest in spirit of contemporary American novelists. Though what he saw in society was always refracted through his own self, was always tangential to his own situation and his private agony, the force behind that agony broke through, enveloped and absorbed the life of contemporary society, as no social realist of the time, not even Dos Passos, ever did. He had come to believe that the Enemy was as much the nemesis of his America as it was of himself; and in that identification lay half his strength, and as has too often been forgotten, something as representative of his spirit as his lack of artistic discipline.

In one sense, then, there were two forces in Wolfe, mutually accommodating, springing from the same source, yet different in tone and effect. One was the mountaineer's son who wrote with a hard, driving force of the people he had hated as a child, who described the death of Old Gant, the peregrinations of Bascom Hawke, his mother's haggard kitchen sourness and scolding old age —the Wolfe who poured into the first third of *The Web and the Rock* a beautiful and haunting chronicle of mountain legends and mountain life, the Wolfe who composed a whole gallery of titanic American portraits and, almost with his last breath, sketched the decomposition of the German soul preparing itself for Fascism in *You Can't Go Home Again*. It was the Wolfe who proved himself a richly comic novelist, with an ear for dialogue, a sense of timing (consider the reproduction of the gasping, stammering Gant speech in the first chapter of *Of Time and the River,* the fantastic montage of New York in all his last works, the Brooklyn scenes in *You*

*Can't Go Home Again*) that were remarkable in their nervous power. It was the Wolfe who wrote the unforgettable sketch of the New York poor huddling in the City Hall latrine for warmth in the depth of a depression winter, the creator of Nebraska Crane and "Lloyd McHarg" and Ben Gant and Grover. He saw them always —Hitler Germany and the baseball players out of his boyhood, the Jewish students at "The School for Utility Cultures" and Esther Jack, the mountain folk and Foxhall Edwards—as segments of that outer world that had significance only in its relation to Eugene Gant-George Webber, saw them often with a disproportionate intensity and strident wit that were literally fantastic in their excess; but he saw them always with great acuteness and wit, and they became, for all their stridency or angularity, as vivid and true as he had seen them in his mind.

The "other" Wolfe, always the centripetal Wolfe who related everything to the dead center of his own fate, was the Asheville, North Carolina Hamlet who dramatized himself perpetually in pride and suffering, rose in his books above the world he was trying to discover and redeem, and could never save himself. For at the bottom of all his frenzy, his herculean misery, the millions of words that spurted out of his pen without drawing him closer to the salvation, the answer he needed so desperately, lay an extraordinary fear of himself and the world he lived in. He was proud of his passion, he even gloried in its energy; but it could not satisfy him. Jason and Kronos, Orestes and Faust, as he proclaimed himself in *Of Time and the River,* he was also a gangling overgrown boy with seven brothers and sisters whose mother kept a boardinghouse in Asheville, and whose father was a stonecutter with a taste for rhetoric. He had been mocked as a child, had been awakened on cold winter mornings to deliver newspapers (lost, lost, forever lost), and had suffered like a million other American boys (but so much more than they) because his parents were dull, his gifts unrecognized, and his teachers stupid. The stonecutter's son had gone on to college, self-conscious before the middle-class campus nobility; he was no good at baseball, he had a taste for Elizabethan prose, and he was vaguely rumored to be queer. Later he went to Harvard, wrote plays, and came to New York to dazzle the stage. Instead, he became a college instructor. His classes were full of gossipy, hungry, loud, and superficial children who stared at him, who did not love the best that had been thought and said, and whose greatest ambition was to become Certified Public Accountants.

Wolfe raged and suffered; he was lonely, he prowled the streets of New York, hated the beast-city and the beast-people, wept, and thought himself a failure. At night he wrote savagely in old ledgers, and wrote always of himself; he would reclaim the dream of time lost in the Rock City, he would make himself a monument. *"Could I make tongue say more than tongue could utter! Could I make brain grasp more than brain could think! Could I weave into immortal denseness some small brede of words, pluck out of sunken depths the roots of living, some hundred thousand magic words that were as great as all my hunger, and hurl the sum of all my living out upon three hundred pages!"* That Wolfe was the Tarzan of rhetoric, the noble lover, the antagonist of cities, the spear of fate, the Wolfe whose rhetoric, swollen with archaisms out of the English classics, can be as painful to read as a child's scrawlings. His rhetoric, pilfered recklessly from the Jacobeans and Sir Thomas Browne, James Joyce and Swinburne, Gilbert Murray and the worst traditions of Southern oratory, was a gluttonous English instructor's accumulation. He became enraptured with the altitudinous, ceremonial prose of the seventeenth century, with the vague splendors of a dozen assorted romanticisms, and united them at the pitch of his father's mountain oratory. Yet it is significant that the more Wolfe sank into the bog of "lost, ah forever lost," "the fairest fame of praise," "a thousand barren and desolate places, a thousand lights and weathers of the soul's gray horror," "he was the Lord of life, the master of the earth, he was the city's conqueror," the more did he seek refuge not in what he felt but in celebrating his own uncertainty, in giving epic grandeur to his own frustration. He wrote his private rhetoric because he had no faith in that writing; he repeated himself, rang endless euphuistic variations on the same phrase, embossed it. As he wrote on and on, he yielded to his confusion and embraced it; it came to hold a music for him, for in the very statement of his wretchedness, with its emotion and nervous clamor, he found the tonal equivalent of his spaceless and inchoate ambition.

In his first works, notably *Look Homeward, Angel,* this rhetoric was almost cheerfully self-conscious, a facile clouded magnificence, and transparently bookish—"Holding in fief the storm and the dark and all the black powers of wizardry, to gaze, ghoul-visaged, through a storm-lashed window-pane, briefly planting unutterable horror in grouped and sheltered life." The two most obvious influences upon the book, curiously enough, seem to have been Sinclair Lewis and James Joyce, and it is the tension of this divided loyalty that makes the novel seem the most cheerfully "objective" of Wolfe's novels, full of a folksy, quasi-poetic braggadocio in the worst and best style of Lewis, and yet the most confusedly romantic. At one point he even inserted a literal reproduction of the Joycean stream-of-consciousness soliloquy, and much of the bad poetry of the book came from his desire to imitate the silken mellifluousness of Joyce's prose lyrics in *A Portrait of the Artist as a Young Man*. Yet for all its tense imitativeness and mawkishness, that first novel seems in retrospect to have been Wolfe's least harried production, and curiously "objective," if only because he was attempting to describe a period in his life that he felt completely behind him. Later, for all his more significant achievements, the prose became more obviously expansive, and even mechanical, in its self-indulgence; it seemed to be fixed in perpetual attitudes of defiance and supplication, where the author of *Look Homeward, Angel*, describing his earliest youth, was commemorating his adolescent exaltations with a certain detachment and what was almost passing good humor.

For by the time he had completed and published *Of Time and the River*, six years after the publication of his first novel, Wolfe had caught up with his life, or rather had not caught up with it at all. His books and his life became so indistinguishably confused that his novels and stories became the living record of every phase in his experience and formed his journal. When, as it was frequently announced toward the end of his life, he "changed" in the direction of a greater maturity and objective comprehension, he never ceased to portray everything in American (and European) society as an accompaniment to, or a variation upon, the rhythm of his psychic life; he had reached that point in his novel-journal where the events of his own life had become contemporaneous with the depression and the impending Second World War. It was at the moment of his greatest agony, therefore, that he found himself reporting the contemporary crisis between Black Friday, 1929, and Munich; and reporting it as that larger history of national and international disintegration of which he felt himself a part. For though he did grow in power, grew to the very end, he never attained certainty or the simple confidence that he had found his place in the world and could enjoy some basic relation to it. The great dissolution in America had begun the year he published his first book, 1929, the year of his emergence and reputation; yet his sudden fame crystallized his unhappiness, set up new tensions in his life, as nothing else had. He suddenly realized, in those years when he was wandering in Germany and England, suffering his affair with the Esther Jack in whose world he could not believe, that the publication of his book, the literal proclamation of his self, had not destroyed the old enemy or given him an advantage over it, but had rather caused it to react with a formidable directness and violence against him. He had forgotten, in his basic self-absorption, how cruelly and even selfishly he had described the world of his childhood and youth, as he had forgotten the external significance of his relation to the world at all; and it all came back —at a time when bitterness and hate were rising in the atmosphere like mercury in the glass.

*You Can't Go Home Again,* his last novel, was pieced together out of fragments he left at his death; but for all its gaps and editorial interpolations it did represent this last and most fateful period in Wolfe's life faithfully. He had reached the end, as in his mind America and the world had reached the end, and for all his talk of "going on," of writing "greater and greater," he almost unconsciously told what he wished most to tell when he wrote into the fragments of the book a long study in dissolution. For *You Can't Go Home Again,* a climax to the one long book he wrote all his life, was rooted in a conviction of decline and fall, of emptiness and dissolution—George Webber himself, Lloyd McHarg, the depression atmosphere in Brooklyn and "Libya Hill," the symbolic party given by Esther and her husband (a bacchanal disturbed by Wagnerian fire), the smashup of his affair with Esther, Germany on the eve of Hitler, the days he spent in a Munich hospital after a brawl. And since he was writing with something more than his old fury, with what seemed almost a new sense of prophecy and scorn,

he was able to invest the poverty of New York, the crash back
home, the bitterness his family and old neighbors felt against him,
the very boom psychology of business itself as he saw it rotting
away before him, with a terrible and incandescent loathing.

Something of the old romantic naïveté, always implicit in the
absolute conflict he posed between the world and himself, remained
to the end, as when he wrote of the sudden humiliation of the middle-class "successes" at home that "he had found out something
about life that he had not known before." Yet that naïveté, as always, was the source of half his power. "They were always talking
about the better life that lay ahead of them and of the greater city
they would build," he wrote of the ruined business people in his
old town after the first shock of the depression, "but to George it
seemed that in all such talk there was evidence of a strange and
savage hunger that drove them on, and there was a desperate quality in it, as though what they really hungered for was ruin and
death. It seemed to him that they *were* ruined, and that even when
they laughed and shouted and smote each other on the back, the
knowledge of their ruin was in them." Discovering the external
world afresh at every moment, he discovered what more mature
writers had known perhaps almost too well to say. A raging naïf
to the end, Wolfe had the naïve curiosity as well as the naïve cre-
dulity and bombast; and that curiosity enabled him to see the depression and its atmosphere as a type of universal experience, a
cataclysm not merely rooted in the facts of social change but in-
expressibly more significant than them. He was discovering the
mass agony as he had hitherto explored only his own, and though
that larger world was still only a reflection of his own, he proved,
almost by the depth of his self-absorption, that his romantic conception of a world that seemed to exist only to oppress Thomas
Wolfe *had* actually led him somewhere, had justified his stricken
devotion to Thomas Wolfe and his fate.

The two worlds had converged at last, if only in that last projection of himself which he offered to the world and the Enemy.
And having achieved that much of the essential victory, he proved
—it seems at once so little and so much—that in making his "I"
equal to all America, he could speak for that essential truth in it
which only a certain spirit could know, and suffer. "I believe that

we are lost here in America, but I believe that we shall be found.
. . . I think that the true discovery of America is before us. I think
the true fulfillment of our spirit, of our people, of our mighty and
immortal land, is yet to come." The failure and triumph went hand
in hand to the end, the nonsense and grandeur; and more than he
knew—was not *this* his distinction?—they were his alone. He went
roaring through a world he had never made and which he never
fully understood; a gargantuan boy (they had told him he was different, and he believed it; they told him he was queer and alone,
and he affirmed it), begging, out of that loneliness and secret defeat
—*Believe! Believe!*

# The Sorrows of Thomas Wolfe

## by John Peale Bishop

Thomas Wolfe is dead. And that big work which he was prepared to write, which was to have gone to six long volumes and covered in the course of its narrative the years between 1781 and 1933, with a cast of characters whose numbers would have run into the hundreds, will never be finished. The title which he had chosen for it, *Of Time and the River*, had already been allowed to appear on the second volume. There its application is not altogether clear; how appropriate it would have been to the work as a whole we can only conjecture. No work of such magnitude has been projected by another of his generation in America; Wolfe's imagination, it appears, could conceive on no smaller scale. He was, he confesses, devoted to chance; he had no constant control over his faculties; but his fecundity was nothing less than prodigious. He had, moreover, a tenacity which must, but for his dying, have carried him through to the end.

Dying, he left behind him a mass of manuscript; how much of it can be published there is now no knowing. Wolfe was the most wasteful of writers.

His aim was to set down America as far as it can belong to the experience of one man. Wolfe came early on what was for him the one available truth about this continent—that it was contained in himself. There was no America which could not be made out—mountains, rivers, trains, cities, people—in the memory of an American. If the contours were misty, then they must be made clear. It was in flight from a certain experience of America, as unhappy as it had been apparently sterile, it was in Paris, in an alien land, that

Wolfe first understood with hate and with love the horror and the wonder of his native country. He had crossed the seas from West to East only to come upon the North Carolina hills where he had been born. "I had found out," he says, "during those years that the way to discover one's own country was to leave it; that the way to find America was to find it in one's own heart, one's memory, and one's spirit, and in a foreign land. I think I may say that I discovered America during those years abroad out of my very need of her."

This is not an uncommon experience, but what made it rewarding in Wolfe's case was that his memory was anything but common. He could—and it is the source of what is most authentic in his talents—displace the present so completely by the past that its sights and sounds all but destroyed surrounding circumstance. He then lost the sense of time. For Wolfe, sitting at a table on a terrace in Paris, contained within himself not only the America he had known; he also held, within his body, both his parents. They were there, not only in his memory, but more portentously in the make-up of his mind. They loomed so enormous to him that their shadows fell across the Atlantic, their shade was on the café table under which he stretched his long American legs.

"The quality of my memory," he said in his little book, *The Story of a Novel,* "is characterized, I believe, in a more than ordinary degree by the intensity of its sense impressions, its power to evoke and bring back the odors, sounds, colors, shapes and feel of things with concrete vividness." That is true. But readers of Wolfe will remember that the mother of Eugene Gant was afflicted with what is known as total recall. Her interminable narratives were the despair of her family. Wolfe could no more than Eliza Gant suppress any detail, no matter how irrelevant; indeed, it was impossible for him to feel that any detail was irrelevant to his purpose. The readers of *Look Homeward, Angel* will also remember that Eugene's father had a gift, unrivalled among his associates, of vigorous utterance. Nobody, they said, can tie a knot in the tail of the English language like old W. O. But the elder Gant's speech, for all that it can on occasion sputter into fiery intensity, more often than not runs off into a homespun rhetoric. It sounds strong, but it has very little connection with any outer reality and is meaningless, except in so far as it serves to convey his rage and frustration. We cannot avoid supposing that Wolfe drew these two characters after his own parents. At the time he began writing *Look Homeward, Angel,* he stood far enough apart from them to use the endlessness of Eliza's unheard discourses, the exaggerated violence of old Gant's objurgations, for comic effect. He makes father and mother into something at once larger and less than human. But in his own case, he could not, at least so long as he was at his writing, restrain either the course of his recollections or their outcome in words. He wrote as a man possessed. Whatever was in his memory must be set down— not merely because he was Eliza's son, but because the secret end of all his writing was expiation—and it must be set down in words to which he constantly seems to be attaching more meaning than they can properly own. It was as though he were aware that his novel would have no meaning that could not be found in the words. The meaning of a novel should be in its structure. But in Wolfe's novel, as far as it has gone, it is impossible to discover any structure at all.

## II.

It is impossible to say what Wolfe's position in American letters would have been had he lived to bring his work to completion. At the moment he stands very high in the estimation both of the critics and of the common reader. From the time of *Look Homeward, Angel,* he was regarded, and rightly, as a young man of incomparable promise. *Of Time and the River* seemed to many to have borne out that promise and, since its faults were taken as due merely to an excess of fecundity, it was met with praise as though it were the consummation of all Wolfe's talents. Yet the faults are fundamental. The force of Wolfe's talents is indubitable; yet he did not find for that novel, nor do I believe he could ever have found, a structure of form which would have been capable of giving shape and meaning to his emotional experience. He was not without intelligence; but he could not trust his intelligence, since for him to do so would have been to succumb to conscience. And it was conscience, with its convictions of guilt, that he was continually trying to elude.

His position as an artist is very like that of Hart Crane. Crane was born in 1899, Wolfe in 1900, so that they were almost of an age. Both had what we must call genius; both conceived that genius had been given them that they might celebrate, the one in poetry, the other in prose, the greatness of their country. But Wolfe no more than Crane was able to give any other coherence to his work than that which comes from the personal quality of his writing. And he found, as Crane did before him, that the America he longed to celebrate did not exist. He could record, and none better, its sights, its sounds, and its odors, as they can be caught in a moment of time; he could try, as the poet of *The Bridge* did, to absorb that moment and endow it with the permanence of a myth. But he could not create a continuous America. He could not, for all that he was prepared to cover one hundred and fifty of its years, conceive its history. He can record what comes to his sensibility, but he cannot give us the continuity of experience. Everything for Wolfe is in the moment; he can so try to impress us with the immensity of the moment that it will take on some sort of transcendental meaning. But what that meaning is, escapes him, as it does us. And once it has passed from his mind, he can do nothing but recall another moment, which as it descends into his memory seems always about to deliver itself, by a miracle, of some tremendous import.

Both Crane and Wolfe belonged to a world that is indeed living from moment to moment. And it is because they voice its breakdown in the consciousness of continuity that they have significance for it.

Of the two, Wolfe, I should say, was the more aware of his plight. He was, he tells us, while writing *Of Time and the River,* tormented by a dream in which the sense of guilt was associated with the forgetting of time. "I was unable to sleep, unable to subdue the tumult of these creative energies, and, as a result of this condition, for three years I prowled the streets, explored the swarming web of the million-footed city and came to know it as I had never done before. . . . Moreover, in this endless quest and prowling of the night through the great web and jungle of the city, I saw, lived, felt and experienced the full weight of that horrible human calamity. [The time was that of the bottom of the depression, when Wolfe was living in Brooklyn.] And from it all has come as a final deposit, a burning memory, a certain evidence of the fortitude of man, his ability to suffer and somehow survive. And it is for this reason now that I think I shall always remember this black period with a kind of joy that I could not at that time have believed possible, for it was during this time that I lived my life through to a first completion, and through the suffering and labor of my own life came to share those qualities in the lives of the people around me."

This passage is one of extreme interest, not only for what it tells us of Wolfe at this time, but for the promise it contains of an emotional maturity. For as far as Wolfe had carried the history of Eugene Gant, he was dealing with a young man whose isolation from his fellow men was almost complete. Eugene, and we must suppose the young Wolfe, was incarcerated in his own sensibility. Locked in his cell, he awaits the coming of every moment, as though it would bring the turning of a releasing key. He waits like Ugolino, when he woke uncertain because of his dream and heard not the opening, but the closing of the lock. There is no release. And the place of Wolfe's confinement, no less than that of Ugolino, deserves to be called Famine.

It can be said of Wolfe, as Allen Tate has said of Hart Crane, that he was playing a game in which any move was possible, because none was compulsory. There is no idea which would serve as discipline to the event. For what Wolfe tells us was the idea that furiously pursued him during the composition of *Of Time and the River,* the search for a father, can scarcely be said to appear in the novel, or else it is so incidentally that it seems to no purpose. It does not certainly, as the same search on the part of Stephen Dedalus does in *Ulysses,* prepare a point toward which the whole narrative moves. There was nothing indeed in Wolfe's upbringing to make discipline acceptable to him. He acts always as though his own capacity for feeling, for anguished hope and continual frustration, was what made him superior, as no doubt, along with his romantic propensity for expression, it was. But he was wrong in assuming that those who accept any form of discipline are therefore lacking in vigor. He apparently did not understand that there are those who might say with Yeats, "I could recover if I shrieked my heart's agony," and yet like him are dumb "from human dignity." And his failure to understand was due to no fault of the intelligence, but to a lack of love. The Gant family always strikes us, with its howls of rage, its loud Hah-hahs of hate and derision, as something less than human. And Eugene is a Gant. While in his case we are ready to admit that genius is a law unto itself, we have every right to demand that it discover its own law.

Again like Crane, Wolfe failed to see that at the present time so extreme a manifestation of individualism could not but be morbid. Both came too late into a world too mechanic; they lacked a wilderness and constantly tried to create one as wild as their hearts. It was all very well for them, since both were in the way of being poets, to start out to proclaim the grandeur of America. Such a task seemed superb. But both were led at last, on proud romantic feet, to Brooklyn. And what they found there they abhorred.

They represent, each in his way, a culmination of the romantic spirit in America. There was in both a tremendous desire to impose the will on experience. Wolfe had no uncommon will. And Crane's was strong enough to lead him deliberately to death by drowning. For Wolfe the rewards of experience were always such that he was turned back upon himself. Isolated in his sensations, there was no way out. He continually sought for a door, and there was really none, or only one, the door of death.

## III.

The intellectual labor of the artist is properly confined to the perception of relations. The conscience of the craftsman must see that these relations are so presented that in spite of all complications they are ultimately clear. It is one of the conditions of art that they cannot be abstractly stated, but must be presented to the senses.

What we have at the center of all Wolfe's writing is a single character, and it was certainly the aim of that writing to present this character in all his manifold contacts with the world of our time. Eugene has, we are told, the craving of a Faust to know all experience, to be able to record all the races and all the social classes which may be said to exist in America. Actually Eugene's experience is not confined to America.

But when we actually come to consider Eugene closely, we see that, once he is beyond the overwhelming presence of his family, his contacts with other people are all casual. The perfect experience for Eugene is to see someone in the throes of an emotion which he can imagine, but in which he has no responsible part. From one train, he sees people passing in another train, which is moving at a faster speed than his own.

"And they looked at one another for a moment, they passed and vanished and were gone forever, yet it seemed to him that he had known these people, that he knew them far better than the people in his own train, and that, having met them for an instant under immense and timeless skies, as they were hurled across the continent to a thousand destinations, they had met, passed, vanished, yet would remember this forever. And he thought the people in the two trains felt this, also: slowly they passed each other now, and their mouths smiled and their eyes grew friendly, but he thought there was some sorrow and regret in what they felt. For having lived together as strangers in the immense and swarming city, they had now met upon the everlasting earth, hurled past each other for a moment between two points of time upon the shining rails; never to meet, to speak, to know each other any more, and the briefness of their days, the destiny of man, was in that instant greeting and farewell."

He sees from a train a boy trying to decide to go after a girl; wandering the streets of New York, he sees death come to four men; through one of his students at the university, he comes in contact with an old Jewess wailing a son dead for a year. Each of these moments is completely done; most of them, indeed, overwrought. From the country seen from a train he derives "a wild and solemn joy—the sense of nameless hope, impossible desire, and man's tragic brevity." He reacts to most circumstances, it must seem to us, excessively. But to men and women he does not really answer. The old Jewess's grief fills him "with horror, anger, a sense of cruelty, disgust, and pity." The passion aroused returns to himself. And it is precisely because his passions cannot attain their object, and in one person know peace, that he turns in rage and desire toward the millions. There is in Eugene every emotion you wish but one; there is no love.

The most striking passages in Wolfe's novels always represent these moments of comprehension. For a moment, but a moment only, there is a sudden release of compassion, when some aspect of suffering and bewildered humanity is seized, when the other's emotion is in a timeless completion known. Then the moment passes, and compassion fails. For Eugene Gant, the only satisfactory relationship with another human creature is one which can have no continuity. For the boy at the street corner, seen in the indecision of youthful lust, he has only understanding and pity; the train from which he looks moves on and nothing more is required of Eugene. But if he should approach that same boy on the street, if he should come close enough to overhear him, he would hear only the defilement of language, words which would awaken in him only hate and disgust. He would himself become lonely, strange and cruel. For emotions such as these, unless they can be used with the responsibility of the artist, must remain a torment to the man.

The only human relationship which endures is that of the child to his family. And that is inescapable; once having been, it cannot cease to be. His father is still his father, though dying; and his brother Ben, though dead, remains his brother. He loves and he hates and knows why no more than the poet he quotes. What he does know is that love has been forbidden him.

The only contemporary literary influence on Wolfe which was at all strong is that of Joyce. I shall consider it here only to note that while we know that Joyce could only have created Stephen Dedalus out of the conflicts of his own youth, we never think of Stephen simply as the young Joyce, any more than we think of Hamlet as Shakespeare. He is a creation. But in Wolfe's novels it is impossible to feel that the central figure has any existence apart from the author. He is called Eugene Gant, but that does not deceive any one for a moment; he is, beyond all doubt, Thomas Wolfe. There is, however, one important distinction to be made between them, and one which we should not allow ourselves to forget: Eugene Gant is always younger, by at least ten years, than Thomas Wolfe.

Wolfe described *Of Time and the River* as being devoted to "the period of wandering and hunger in a man's youth." And in it we are meant to take Eugene as every young man. The following volume would, Wolfe said, declare "a period of greater certitude, which would be dominated by a single passion." That, however, still remains to be seen. So far, Eugene has shown no capacity as a lover, except in casual contact with whores. When for a moment he convinces himself that he is in love with Ann, who is a nice, simple conventional girl from Boston, he can only shriek at her and call her a bitch and a whore, which she certainly is not. The one contact which lasts for any time—leaving aside the blood ties which bind him to the Pentlands, his mother's people, and the Gants— is that with Starwick. Starwick is the only friend he makes in his two years at Harvard, and in Paris, some years later, he still regards his friendship with Starwick as the most valuable he has ever known.

It ends when he discovers that Starwick is a homosexual. And it has usually been assumed that the violence and bitterness with which it ends are due to disillusionment; the sudden turn in Eugene's affections for the young man may well be taken as a natural reaction to his learning, first that Ann is in love with Starwick, and only a little later how hopelessly deep is Starwick's infatuation with the young tough he has picked up, by apparent chance, one night in a Paris bar. But that is, I think, to take too simple a view of the affair. There is more to it than that. What we have been told about Starwick from his first appearance in the book is that, despite a certain affection and oddity of manner, he is, as Eugene is not, a person capable of loving and being loved. What is suddenly revealed in Paris is that for him, too, love is a thing the world has forbidden. In Starwick's face Eugene sees his own fate. Just as in his brother Ben's complaint at his neglect, he had looked back through another's sight at his own neglected childhood and in his brother's death foremourned his own, so now, when he beats Starwick's head against the wall, he is but raging against his own frustration and despair.

In his father's yard, among the tombstones, stood for years a marble angel. Old Gant curses it, all hope he thinks lost that he will ever get his money back for it. It stands a magnificent reminder of the time when as a boy, with winged ambition, he had wanted to be not merely a stone cutter but a sculptor. Then, unexpectedly, a customer comes for it. The one symbol of the divine in the workshop is sold to adorn the grave of a prostitute; what the boy might have been the man lets go for such a purpose. It cannot be said that Thomas Wolfe ever sold his angel. But the faults of the artist are all of them traceable to the failures of the man. He achieved probably the utmost intensity of which incoherent writing is capable; he proved that an art founded solely on the individual, however strong his will, however vivid his sensations, cannot be sound, or whole, or even passionate, in a world such as ours, in which "the integrity of the individual consciousness has been broken down." How far it has broken down, I do not believe he ever knew, yet all that he did is made of its fragments.

# Genius Is Not Enough

## by Bernard DeVoto

Some months ago *The Saturday Review* serialized Mr. Thomas Wolfe's account of the conception, gestation, and as yet uncompleted delivery of his Novel, and Scribner's are now publishing the three articles as a book. It is one of the most appealing books of our time. No one who reads it can doubt Mr. Wolfe's complete dedication to his job or regard with anything but respect his attempt to describe the dark and nameless fury of the million-footed life swarming in his dark and unknown soul. So honest or so exhaustive an effort at self-analysis in the interest of esthetics has seldom been made in the history of American literature, and "The Story of a Novel" is likely to have a long life as a source-book for students of literature and for psychologists as well. But also it brings into the public domain material that has been hitherto outside the privilege of criticism. Our first essay must be to examine it in relation to Mr. Wolfe's novels, to see what continuities and determinants it may reveal, and to inquire into their bearing on the art of fiction.

Let us begin with one of many aspects of Mr. Wolfe's novels that impress the reader, the frequent recurrence of material to which one must apply the adjective placental. (The birth metaphors are imposed by Mr. Wolfe himself. In "The Story of a Novel" he finds himself big with first a thunder cloud and then a river. The symbolism of waters is obviously important to him, and the title of his latest novel is to be that of the series as a whole.) A great part of

"'Genius Is Not Enough," by Bernard DeVoto. From *Saturday Review of Literature* xiii (April 25, 1936), pp. 3-4, 13-14. Reprinted by permission of Mrs. Bernard DeVoto, owner of copyright.

This essay was written as a review of *The Story of A Novel* (New York: Charles Scribner's Sons, 1936).

"Look Homeward, Angel" was just the routine first-novel of the period, which many novelists had published and many others had suppressed, the story of a sensitive and rebellious adolescent who was headed toward the writing of novels. The rest of it was not so easily catalogued. Parts of it showed intuition, understanding, and ecstasy, and an ability to realize all three in character and scene, whose equal it would have been hard to point out anywhere in the fiction of the time. These looked like great talent, and in such passages as the lunchroom scene in the dawn that Mr. Wolfe called nacreous some fifty times, they seemed to exist on both a higher and a deeper level of realization than any of Mr. Wolfe's contemporaries had attained. But also there were parts that looked very dubious indeed—long, whirling discharges of words, unabsorbed in the novel, unrelated to the proper business of fiction, badly if not altogether unacceptably written, raw gobs of emotion, aimless and quite meaningless jabber, claptrap, belches, grunts, and Tarzanlike screams. Their rawness, their unshaped quality, must be insisted upon; it was as if the birth of the novel had been accompanied by a lot of the material that had nourished its gestation. The material which nature and most novelists discard when its use has been served. It looked like one of two things, there was no telling which. It looked like the self-consciously literary posturing of a novelist too young and too naive to have learned his trade. Or, from another point of view, it looked like a document in psychic disintegration. And one of the most important questions in contemporary literature was: would the proportion of fiction to placenta increase or decrease in Mr. Wolfe's next book?

It decreased. If fiction of the quality of that lunchroom scene made up about one-fifth of "Look Homeward, Angel," it constituted, in "Of Time and the River," hardly more than a tenth. The placental material had enormously grown and, what was even more ominous, it now had a rationalization. It was as unshaped as before, but it had now been retroactively associated with the dark and nameless heaving of the voiceless and unknown womb of Time, and with the unknown and voiceless fury of the dark and lonely and lost America. There were still passages where Mr. Wolfe was a novelist not only better than most of his contemporaries but altogether out of their class. But they were pushed farther apart and even diluted when they occurred by this dark substance which may have been nameless but was certainly far from voiceless.

Certain other aspects of the new book seemed revealing. For one thing, there was a shocking contempt of the medium. Some passages were not completely translated from the "I" in which they had apparently been written to the "he" of Eugene Gant. Other passages alluded to incidents which had probably appeared in an earlier draft but could not be found in the final one. Others contradictorily reported scenes which had already appeared, and at least once a passage that had seen service already was re-enlisted for a second hitch in a quite different context, apparently with no recollection that it had been used before.

Again, a state of mind that had been appropriate to the puberty of Eugene seemed inappropriate as the boy grew older, and might therefore be significant. I mean the giantism of the characters. Eugene himself, in "Of Time and the River," was clearly a borderline manic-depressive: he exhibited the classic cycle in his alternation between "fury" and "despair," and the classic accompaniment of obsessional neurosis in the compulsions he was under to read all the books in the world, see all the people in Boston, observe all the lives of the man-swarm, and list all the names and places in America. That was simple enough, but practically every other character in the book also suffered from fury and compulsions; and, what was more suggestive, they were all twenty feet tall, spoke with the voice of trumpets and the thunder, ate like Pantagruel, wept like Niobe, laughed like Falstaff, and bellowed like the bulls of Bashan. The significant thing was that we were seeing them all through Eugene's eyes. To a child all adults are giants: their voices are thunderous, their actions are portentous and grotesquely magnified, and all their exhibited emotions are seismic. It looked as if part of Eugene's condition was an infantile regression.

This appearance was reinforced by what seemed to be another stigma of infantilism: that all the experiences in "Of Time and the River" were on the same level and had the same value. When Mr. Gant died (of enough cancer to have exterminated an army corps), the reader accepted the accompanying frenzy as proper to the death of a man's father—which is one of the most important events in anyone's life. But when the same frenzy accompanied nearly everything else in the book—a ride on a railroad train, a literary tea-fight, a midnight lunch in the kitchen, a quarrel between friends, a walk at night, the rejection of a play, an automobile trip, a seduction that misfired, the discovery of Eugene's true love—one could only decide that something was dreadfully wrong. If the death of one's father comes out emotionally even with a ham-on-rye, then the art of fiction is cockeyed.

Well, "The Story of a Novel" puts an end to speculation and supplies some unexpected but very welcome light. To think of these matters as contempt of the medium, regression, and infantilism is to be too complex and subtle. The truth shows up in two much simpler facts: that Mr. Wolfe is still astonishingly immature, and that he has mastered neither the psychic material out of which a novel is made nor the technique of writing fiction. He does not seem aware of the first fact, but he acknowledges the second with a frankness and an understanding that are the finest promise to date for his future books. How far either defect is reparable it is idle to speculate. But at least Mr. Wolfe realizes that he is, as yet, by no means a complete novelist.

The most flagrant evidence of his incompleteness is the fact that, so far, one indispensable part of the artist has existed not in Mr. Wolfe but in Maxwell Perkins. Such organizing faculty and such critical intelligence as have been applied to the book have come not from inside the artist, not from the artist's feeling for form and esthetic integrity, but from the office of Charles Scribner's Sons. For five years the artist pours out words "like burning lava from a volcano"—with little or no idea what their purpose is, which book they belong in, what the relation of part to part is, what is organic and what irrelevant, or what emphasis or coloration in the completed work of art is being served by the job at hand. Then Mr. Perkins decides these questions—from without, and by a process to which rumor applies the word "assembly." But works of art cannot be assembled like a carburetor—they must be grown like a plant, or in Mr. Wolfe's favorite simile, like an embryo. The artist writes a hundred thousand words about a train: Mr. Perkins decides that the train is worth only five thousand words. But such a decision as this is properly not within Mr. Perkins's power; it must be made by the highly conscious self-criticism of the artist in relation to the pulse of the book itself. Worse still, the artist goes on writing till Mr. Perkins tells him that the novel is finished. But the end of a novel is, properly, dictated by the internal pressure, osmosis, metabolism—what you will—of the novel itself, of which only the novelist can have a first-hand knowledge. There comes a point where the necessities of the book are satisfied, where its organic processes have reached completion. It is hard to see how awareness of that point can manifest itself at an editor's desk—and harder still to trust the integrity of a work of art in which not the artist but the publisher has determined where the true ends and the false begins.

All this is made more ominous by Mr. Wolfe's almost incredibly youthful attitude toward revision. No novel is written till it is revised—the process is organic, it is one of the processes of art. It is, furthermore, the process above all others that requires objectivity, a feeling for form, a knowledge of what the necessities of the book are, a determination that those necessities shall outweigh and dominate everything else. It is, if not the highest functioning of the artistic intelligence, at least a fundamental and culminating one. But the process appears to Mr. Wolfe not one which will free his book from falsity, irrelevance, and its private incumbrances, not one which will justify and so exalt the artist—but one that makes his spirit quiver "at the bloody execution" and his soul "recoil from the carnage of so many lovely things." But superfluous and mistaken things are lovely to only a very young writer, and the excision of them is bloody carnage only if the artist has not learned to subdue his ego in favor of his book. And the same juvenility makes him prowl "the streets of Paris like a maddened animal" because—for God's sake!—the reviewers may not like the job.

The placental passages are now explained. They consist of psychic material which the novelist has proved unable to shape into fiction. The failure may be due either to immature understanding or to insufficient technical skill: probably both causes operate here and cannot be separated. The principle is very simple. When Mr. Wolfe gives us his doctors, undertakers, and newspapermen talking in a lunchroom at dawn, he does his job—magnificently. There they are, and the reader revels in the dynamic presentation of human beings, and in something else as well that should have the greatest possible significance for Mr. Wolfe. For while the doctors and undertakers are chaffing one another, the reader gets that feeling of the glamour and mystery of American life which Mr. Wolfe elsewhere unsuccessfully labors to evoke in thousands of rhapsodic words. The novelist makes his point in the lives of his characters, not in tidal surges of rhetoric.

Is America lost, lonely, nameless, and unknown? Maybe, and maybe not. But if it is, the condition of the novelist's medium requires him to make it lost and lonely in the lives of his characters, not in blank verse, bombast, and apocalyptic delirium. You cannot represent America by hurling adjectives at it. Do "the rats of death and age and dark oblivion feed forever at the roots of sleep?" It sounds like a high school valedictory, but if in fact they do then the novelist is constrained to show them feeding so by means of what his characters do and say and feel in relation to one another, and not by chasing the ghosts of Whitman and Ezekiel through fifty pages of disembodied emotion. Such emotion is certainly the material that fiction works with, but until it is embodied in character and scene it is not fiction—it is only logorrhea. A poem should not mean but be, Mr. MacLeish tells us, and poetry is always proving that fundamental. In a homelier aphorism Mr. Cohan has expressed the same imperative of the drama: "Don't tell 'em, show 'em." In the art of fiction the *thing* is not only an imperative, it is a primary condition. A novel *is*—it cannot be asserted, ranted, or even detonated. A novelist represents life. When he does anything else, no matter how beautiful or furious or ecstatic the way in which he does it, he is not writing fiction. Mr. Wolfe can write fiction—has written some of the finest fiction of our day. But a great part of what he writes is not fiction at all: it is only material with which the novelist has struggled but which has defeated him. The most important question in American fiction today, probably, is whether he can win that encounter in his next book. It may be that "The October Fair" and "The Hills Beyond Pentland" will show him winning it, but one remembers the dilution from "Look Homeward, Angel" to "Of Time and the River" and is apprehensive. If he does win it, he must do so inside himself; Mr. Perkins and the assembly line at Scribner's can do nothing to help him.

That struggle has another aspect. A novelist utilizes the mechanism of fantasy for the creation of a novel, and there are three kinds of fantasy with which he works. One of them is unconscious fantasy, about which Dr. Kubie was writing in these columns something over a year ago. A novelist is wholly subject to its emphases and can do nothing whatever about them—though when Mr. Wolfe says that the center of all living is reconciliation with one's father he comes close to revealing its pattern in him. There remain two kinds of fantasy which every novelist employs—but which every one employs in a different ratio. Call them identification and projection, call them automatic and directed, call them proliferating and objectified—the names do not matter. The novelist surrenders himself to the first kind, but dominates and directs the second kind. In the first kind he says "I am Napoleon" and examines himself to see how he feels. In the second kind, he wonders how Napoleon feels, and instead of identifying himself with him, he tries to discover Napoleon's necessities. If he is excessively endowed with the first kind of fantasy, he is likely to be a genius. But if he learns to utilize the second kind in the manifold inter-relationships of a novel he is certain to be an artist. Whatever Mr. Wolfe's future in the wider and looser interest of Literature, his future in the far more rigorous interest of fiction just about comes down to the question of whether he can increase his facility at the second kind of fantasy. People would stop idiotically calling him autobiographical, if he gave us less identification and more understanding. And we could do with a lot less genius, if we got a little more artist.

For the truth is that Mr. Wolfe is presented to us, and to himself, as a genius. There is no more dissent from that judgment in his thinking about himself than in Scribner's publicity. And, what is more, a genius of the good old-fashioned, romantic kind—possessed by a demon, driven by the gales of his own fury, helpless before the lava-flood of his own passion, selected and set apart for greatness, his lips touched by a live coal, consequently unable to exercise any control over what he does and in fact likely to be damaged or diminished by any effort at control. Chaos is everything, if you have enough of it in you to make a world. Yes, but what if you don't make a world—what if you just make a noise? There was chaos in Stephen Dedalus's soul, but he thought of that soul not as sufficient in itself but merely as a smithy wherein he might forge his novel. And listen to Mr. Thomas Mann:

> When I think of the masterpiece of the twentieth century, I have an idea of something that differs essentially and, in my opinion, with profit from the Wagnerian masterpiece—something exceptionally logical, clear, and well developed in form, something at once austere and serene, with no less intensity of will than his, but of cooler, nobler, even healthier spirituality, something that seeks its greatness not in the colossal, the baroque, and its beauty not in intoxication.

Something, in other words, with inescapable form, something which exists as the imposition of order on chaos, something that *is*, not is merely asserted.

One can only respect Mr. Wolfe for his determination to realize himself on the highest level and to be satisfied with nothing short of greatness. But, however useful genius may be in the writing of novels, it is not enough in itself—it never has been enough, in any art, and it never will be. At the very least it must be supported by an ability to impart shape to material, simple competence in the use of tools. Until Mr. Wolfe develops more craftsmanship, he will not be the important novelist he is now widely accepted as being. In order to be a great novelist he must also mature his emotions till he can see more profoundly into character than he now does, and he must learn to put a corset on his prose. Once more: his own smithy is the only possible place for these developments—they cannot occur in the office of any editor whom he will ever know.

# Thomas Wolfe

## by *Maxwell E. Perkins*

I think that there is not in any one place so nearly complete a collection of an author's writings and records as that of Thomas Wolfe's now in the Harvard Library. When he died on that sad day in September 1938, when war was impending, or soon after that, I learned that I was his executor and that he had actually left little—as he would have thought, and as it seemed then—besides his manuscripts. It was my obligation to dispose of them to the advantage of his beneficiaries and his memory, and though the times were bad, and Wolfe had not then been recognized as what he now is, I could have sold them commercially, piecemeal, through dealers, for more money than they ever brought. I was determined that this literary estate should remain a unit, available to writers and students, and I tried to sell it as such; but at that time, with war clouds gathering and soon bursting, I could find no adequate buyer.

Then Aline Bernstein, to whom Wolfe had given the manuscript of *Look Homeward, Angel,* sold it by auction for the relief of her people in misfortune, on the understanding that it would be given to Harvard. Not long after that William B. Wisdom, who had recognized Wolfe as a writer of genius on the publication of the *Angel,* and whose faith in him had never wavered, offered to purchase all of his manuscripts and records. He had already accumulated a notable collection of Wolfiana. His correspondence showed me that he thought as I did—that the point of supreme importance was that these records and writings should not be scattered to the four winds, that they be kept intact. And so the whole great packing case of material—letters, bills, documents, notebooks and manuscripts—

"Thomas Wolfe" by Maxwell Perkins first appeared in *Harvard Library Bulletin,* Volume I (Autumn, 1947) and is reprinted by permission of *Harvard Library Bulletin* and Charles Scribner's Sons. Copyright 1947 by Charles Scribner's Sons.

went to him on the stipulation, which I never need have asked for, that he would will it all to one institution. Since *Look Homeward, Angel,* was already in Harvard, since Tom Wolfe had loved the reading room of the Library where, as he so often told me, he devoured his hundreds of books and spent most of his Harvard years, Mr Wisdom made a gift of all this to Harvard. And there it now is.

Though I had worked as an editor with Thomas Wolfe on two huge manuscripts, *Look Homeward, Angel* and *Of Time and the River,* I was astonished on that Spring evening of 1935 when Tom, about to sail for England, brought to our house on East 49th Street, because Scribner's was closed, the huge packing case containing all his literary material. Tom and I and the taxi man carried it in and set it down. Then Tom said to the man, 'What is your name?' He said, 'Lucky.' 'Lucky!' said Tom—I think it was perhaps an Americanization of some Italian name—and grasped his hand. It seemed a good omen. We three had done something together. We were together for that moment. We all shook hands. But for days, that huge packing case blocked our hall, until I got it removed to Scribner's.

The first time I heard of Thomas Wolfe I had a sense of foreboding. I who loved the man say this. Every good thing that comes is accompanied by trouble. It was in 1928 when Madeleine Boyd, a literary agent, came in. She talked of several manuscripts which did not much interest me, but frequently interrupted herself to tell of a wonderful novel about an American boy. I several times said to her, 'Why don't you bring it in here, Madeleine?' and she seemed to evade the question. But finally she said, 'I will bring it, if you promise to read every word of it.' I did promise, but she told me other things that made me realize that Wolfe was a turbulent spirit, and that we were in for turbulence. When the manuscript came, I was fascinated by the first scene where Eugene's father, Oliver W. Gant, with his brother, two little boys, stood by a roadside in Pennsylvania and saw a division of Lee's Army on the march to Gettysburg.

But then there came some ninety-odd pages about Oliver Gant's life in Newport News, and Baltimore, and elsewhere. All this was what Wolfe had heard, and had no actual association with which to reconcile it, and it was inferior to the first episode, and in fact to all the rest of the book. I was turned off to other work and gave the manuscript to Wallace Meyer, thinking, 'Here is another promising novel that probably will come to nothing.' Then Meyer showed me that wonderful night scene in the cafe where Ben was with the Doctors, and Horse Hines, the undertaker, came in. I dropped everything and began to read again, and all of us were reading the book simultaneously, you might say, including John Hall Wheelock, and there never was the slightest disagreement among us as to its importance.

After some correspondence between me and Wolfe, and between him and Madeleine Boyd, from which we learned how at the October Fair in Germany he had been almost beaten to death—when I realized again that we had a Moby Dick to deal with—Wolfe arrived in New York and stood in the doorway of my boxstall of an office leaning against the door jamb. When I looked up and saw his wild hair and bright countenance—although he was so altogether different physically—I thought of Shelley. *He* was fair, but his hair was wild, and his face was bright and his head disproportionately small.

We then began to work upon the book and the first thing we did, to give it unity, was to cut out that wonderful scene it began with and the ninety-odd pages that followed, because it seemed to me, and he agreed, that the whole tale should be unfolded through the memories and senses of the boy, Eugene, who was born in Asheville. We both thought that the story was compassed by that child's realization; that it was life and the world as he came to realize them. When he had tried to go back into the life of his father before he arrived in Asheville, without the inherent memory of events, the reality and the poignance were diminished—but for years it was on my conscience that I had persuaded Tom to cut out that first scene of the two little boys on the roadside with Gettysburg impending.

And then what happened? In *Of Time and the River* he brought the scene back to greater effect when old Gant was dying on the gallery of the hospital in Baltimore and in memory recalled his olden days. After that occurred I felt much less anxiety in suggesting cuts: I began then to realize that nothing Wolfe wrote was ever lost, that omissions from one book were restored in a later one. An extreme example of this is the fact that the whole second half of *The Web and the Rock* was originally intended to be the concluding episode in *Of Time and the River*. But most, and perhaps almost all, of those early incidents of Gant's life were worked into *The Web and the Rock* and *You Can't Go Home Again*.

I had realized, for Tom had prefaced his manuscript with a statement to that effect, that *Look Homeward, Angel* was autobiographical, but I had come to think of it as being so in the sense that *David Copperfield* is, or *War and Peace,* or *Pendennis*. But when we were working together, I suddenly saw that it was often almost literally autobiographical—that these people in it were his people. I am sure my face took on a look of alarm, and Tom saw it and he said, 'But Mr Perkins, you don't understand. I think these people are *great* people and that they should be told about.' He was right. He had written a great book, and it had to be taken substantially as it was. And in truth, the extent of cutting in that book has somehow come to be greatly exaggerated. Really, it was more a matter of reorganization. For instance, Tom had that wonderful episode when Gant came back from his far-wandering and rode in early morning on the trolley car through the town and heard about who had died and who had been born and saw all the scenes that were so familiar to Tom or Eugene, as the old trolley rumbled along. This was immediately followed by an episode of a similar kind where Eugene, with his friends, walked home from school through the town of Asheville. That was presented in a Joycean way, but it was the same sort of thing—some one going through the town and through his perceptions revealing it to the reader. By putting these episodes next to each other the effect of each was diminished, and I think we gave both much greater value by separating them. We did a great deal of detailed cutting, but it was such things as that I speak of that constituted perhaps the greater part of the work.

*Of Time and the River* was a much greater struggle for Tom. Eventually, I think it was on Thanksgiving Day 1933, he brought me in desperation about two feet of typescript. The first scene in this was the platform of the railroad station in Asheville when Eugene was about to set out for Harvard, and his family had come to see him off. It must have run to about 30,000 words and I cut it to perhaps 10,000 and showed it to Tom. He approved it. When you are

waiting for a train to come in, there is suspense. Something is going
to happen. You must, it seemed to me, maintain that sense of suspense and you can't to the extent of 30,000 words. There never was
any cutting that Tom did not agree to. He knew that cutting was
necessary. His whole impulse was to utter what he felt and he had no
time to revise and compress.

So then we began a year of nights of work, including Sundays, and
every cut, and change, and interpolation, was argued about and
about. The principle that I was working on was that this book, too,
got its unity and its form through the senses of Eugene, and I remember how, if I had had my way, we should, by sticking to that
principle, have lost one of the most wonderful episodes Wolfe ever
wrote—the death of Gant. One night we agreed that certain transi-
tions should be written in, but instead of doing them Wolfe brought
on the next night some five thousand words about Eugene's sister in
Asheville when her father was ill, and a doctor there and a nurse.
I said, 'Tom, this is all outside the story, and you know it. Eugene
was not there, he was in Cambridge; all of this was outside his perception and knowledge at the time.' Tom agreed with me, but the
next night, he brought me another five thousand words or so which
got up into the death of Gant. And then I realized I was wrong, even
if right in theory. What he was doing was too good to let any rule of
form impede him.

It is said that Tolstoy never willingly parted with the manuscript
of *War and Peace*. One could imagine him working on it all through
his life. Certainly Thomas Wolfe never willingly parted from the
proofs of *Of Time and the River*. He sat brooding over them for
weeks in the Scribner library and not reading. John Wheelock read
them and we sent them to the printer and told Tom it had been
done. I could believe that otherwise he might have clung to them
to the end.

He dedicated that book to me in most extravagant terms. I never
saw the dedication until the book was published and though I was
most grateful for it, I had forebodings when I heard of his intention.
I think it was that dedication that threw him off his stride and broke
his magnificent scheme. It gave shallow people the impression that
Wolfe could not function as a writer without collaboration, and one
critic even used some such phrases as, 'Wolfe and Perkins—Perkins

and Wolfe, what way is that to write a novel.' Nobody with the slightest comprehension of the nature of a writer could accept such an assumption. No writer could possibly tolerate the assumption, which perhaps Tom almost himself did, that he was dependent as a writer upon anyone else. He had to prove to himself and to the world that this was not so.

And that was the fundamental reason that he turned to another publisher. If he had not—but by the time he did it was plain that he had to tell, in the medium of fiction and through the transmutation of his amazing imagination, the story of his own life—he never would have broken his own great plan by distorting Eugene Gant into George Webber. That was a horrible mistake. I think Edward Aswell, of Harper & Brothers, agrees with me in this, but when the manuscript that came to form *The Web and the Rock* and *You Can't Go Home Again* got to him to work on, and in some degree to me, as Wolfe's executor, Tom was dead, and things had to be taken as they were.

The trouble began after the publication of *Of Time and the River,* which the reviewers enormously praised—but many of them asserted that Wolfe could only write about himself, that he could not see the world or anything objectively, with detachment—that he was always autobiographical. Wolfe was extremely sensitive to criticism, for all his tremendous faith in his genius as an obligation put upon him to fulfill. One day when I lived on East 49th Street near Second Avenue, and he on First Avenue, just off the corner of 49th, I met him as I was going home. He said he wanted to talk to me, as we did talk every evening about that time, and we went into the Waldorf. He referred to the criticisms against him, and said that he wanted to write a completely objective, unautobiographical book, and that it would show how strangely different everything is from what a person expects it to be. One might say that he was thinking of the theme that has run through so many great books, such as *Pickwick Papers* and *Don Quixote,* where a man, young or old, goes hopefully out into the world slap into the face of outrageous reality. He was going to put on the title page what was said by Prince Andrei, in *War and Peace,* after his first battle, when the praise fell upon those who had done nothing and blame almost fell upon one who had done everything. Prince Andrei, who saved the battery com-

mander who most of all had held back the French from the blame
that Little Tushin would have accepted, walked out with him into
the night. Then as Tushin left, Tolstoy said, 'Prince Andrei looked
up at the stars and sighed; everything was so different from what he
thought it was going to be.'

Tom was in a desperate state. It was not only what the critics said
that made him wish to write objectively, but that he knew that what
he had written had given great pain even to those he loved the most.
The conclusion of our talk was that if he could write such an objective book on this theme within a year, say, to the extent of perhaps a hundred thousand words, it might be well to do it. It was
this that turned him to George Webber, but once he began on that
he really and irresistibly resumed the one story he was destined to
write, which was that of himself, or Eugene Gant.

And so, the first half of *The Web and the Rock*, of which there is
only a typescript, is a re-telling in different terms of *Look Homeward, Angel*. Wolfe was diverted from his natural purpose—and
even had he lived, what could have been done? Some of his finest
writing is that first half of *The Web and the Rock*. Could anybody
have just tossed it out?

But, if Tom had held to his scheme and completed the whole story
of his life as transmuted into fiction through his imagination, I think
the accusation that he had no sense of form could not have stood.
He wrote one long story, 'The Web of Earth,' which had perfect
form, for all its intricacy. I remember saying to him, 'Not one word
of this should be changed.' One might say that as his own physical
dimensions were huge so was his conception of a book. He had one
book to write about a vast, sprawling, turbulent land—America—
as perceived by Eugene Gant. Even when he was in Europe, it was of
America he thought. If he had not been diverted and had lived to
complete it, I think it would have had the form that was suited to
the subject.

His detractors say he could only write about himself, but all that
he wrote of was transformed by his imagination. For instance, in
*You Can't Go Home Again* he shows the character Foxhall Edwards
at breakfast. Edwards's young daughter enters 'as swiftly and silently
as a ray of light.' She is very shy and in a hurry to get to school. She
tells of a theme she has written on Walt Whitman and what the

teacher said of Whitman. When Edwards urges her not to hurry and makes various observations, she says, 'Oh, Daddy, you're so funny!' What Tom did was to make one unforgettable little character out of three daughters of Foxhall Edwards.

He got the ray of light many years ago when he was with me in my house in New Canaan, Connecticut, and one daughter, at the age of about eight or ten, came in and met this gigantic stranger. After she was introduced she fluttered all about the room in her embarrassment, but radiant, like a sunbeam. Then Tom was present when another daughter, in Radcliffe, consulted me about a paper she was writing on Whitman, but he put this back into her school days. The third, of which he composed a single character, was the youngest, who often did say, partly perhaps because she was not at ease when Tom was there, 'Oh, Daddy, you're so silly.' That is how Tom worked. He created something new and something meaningful through a transmutation of what he saw, heard, and realized.

I think no one could understand Thomas Wolfe who had not seen or properly imagined the place in which he was born and grew up. Asheville, N. C., is encircled by mountains. The trains wind in and out through labyrinths of passes. A boy of Wolfe's imagination imprisoned there could think that what was beyond was all wonderful—different from what it was where there was not for him enough of anything. Whatever happened, Wolfe would have been what he was. I remember on the day of his death saying to his sister Mabel that I thought it amazing in an American family that one of the sons who wanted to be a writer should have been given the support that was given Tom, and that they all deserved great credit for that. She said it didn't matter, that nothing could have prevented Tom from doing what he did.

That is true, but I think that those mountainous walls which his imagination vaulted gave him the vision of an America with which his books are fundamentally concerned. He often spoke of the artist in America—how the whole color and character of the country was completely new—never interpreted; how in England, for instance, the writer inherited a long accretion of accepted expression from which he could start. But Tom would say—and he had seen the world—'who has ever made you know the color of an American box car?' Wolfe was in those mountains—he tells of the train whistles at night—the trains were winding their way out into the great world where it seemed to the boy there was everything desirable, and vast, and wonderful.

It was partly that which made him want to see everything, and read everything, and experience everything, and say everything. There was a night when he lived on First Avenue that Nancy Hale, who lived on East 49th Street near Third Avenue, heard a kind of chant, which grew louder. She got up and looked out of the window at two or three in the morning and there was the great figure of Thomas Wolfe, advancing in his long country-man's stride, with his swaying black raincoat, and what he was chanting was, 'I wrote ten thousand words today—I wrote ten thousand words today.'

Tom must have lived in eight or nine different parts of New York and Brooklyn for a year or more. He knew in the end every aspect of the City—he walked the streets endlessly—but he was not a city man. The city fascinated him but he did not really belong in it and was never satisfied to live in it. He was always thinking of America as a whole and planning trips to some part that he had not yet seen, and in the end taking them. His various quarters in town always looked as if he had just moved in, to camp for awhile. This was partly because he really had no interest in possessions of any kind, but it was also because he was in his very nature a Far Wanderer, bent upon seeing all places, and his rooms were just necessities into which he never settled. Even when he was there his mind was not. He needed a continent to range over, actually and in imagination. And his place was all America. It was with America he was most deeply concerned and I believe he opened it up as no other writer ever did for the people of his time and for the writers and artists and poets of tomorrow. Surely he had a thing to tell us.

# The Last Letter of Thomas Wolfe, and the Reply to It

Providence Hospital
17th Avenue and East Jefferson Street
Seattle, Wash.

Aug. 12, 1938

Dear Max: I'm sneaking this against orders—but "I've got a hunch"—and I wanted to write these words to you.

—I've made a long voyage and been to a strange country, and I've seen the dark man very close; and I don't think I was too much afraid of him, but so much of mortality still clings to me—I wanted most desperately to live and still do, and I thought about you all a 1000 times, and wanted to see you all again, and there was the impossible anguish and regret of all the work I had not done, of all the work I had to do—and I know now I'm just a grain of dust, and I feel as if a great window had been opened on life I did not know about before—and if I come through this, I hope to God I am a better man, and in some strange way I can't explain I know I am a deeper and wiser one— If I get on my feet and out of here, it will be months before I [?] back, but if I get on my feet, I'll come back

—Whatever happens—I had this "hunch" and wanted to write you and tell you, no matter what happens or has happened, I shall always think of you and feel about you the way it was that 4th of July day 3 yrs. ago when you met me at the boat, and we went out on the café on the river and had a drink and later went on top of the tall building and all the strangeness and the glory and the power of life and of the city were below—Yours Always

Tom

Aug. 19, 1938

Dear Tom:

I was most happy to get your letter, but don't do it again. That is enough, and will always be valued. And I remember that night as a magical night, and the way the city looked. I always meant to go back there, but maybe it would be better not to, for things are never the same the second time. I tried to find you some good picture books, and found three good in their way. But maybe I shall find something better. I'll keep my eyes open for it.

Everyone hereabouts is greatly concerned over your illness, and that means many people who do not even know you too. Don't get impatient about loss of time. You don't really lose time, in the ordinary sense.— Even six months would not be important. Even if you were really relaxing, as they call it, all that time, you would be getting good from it, even as a writer.—I hope you will manage to do it too.

I am expecting to go up with Louise tomorrow to Windsor, for over Sunday, mostly to see my mother, and to see my uncle who has now passed ninety, and is in better shape than he was ten or twelve years ago. He was next to the oldest in that family of twelve, just barely too young for the Civil War to which his brother ran away, from Yale, and joined the cavalry and got his health destroyed by it, but I think Uncle Ally would have come through that all right. I do not think though, that he is going to cheer me up about the state of the nation and the prospects for the human race. He foretold the downfall of 1929, but said that he did not expect anyone to listen to him. And they didn't.

I could send you some good books to read, but I don't think you will want to do any reading for yet awhile. What you ought to do is to realize that by really resting now, you are in fact actually gaining time, not losing it.

Always yours,

Max

# The Function of Appetite

*by Wright Morris*

Didn't Hemingway say this in effect: if Tom Wolfe ever learns to separate what he gets from books from what he gets from life, he will be an original.

—"Notebooks" F. Scott Fitzgerald

If Tom Wolfe ever learned, he left no evidence of it. He never learned to separate what he got from books from what he got from life. His appetite wouldn't let him. A glutton for life, he actually died of impoverishment. He bolted both life and literature in such a manner he failed to get real nourishment from either. Nothing that he devoured, since it was not digested, satisfied his insatiable appetite. He was aware of that himself, and his now legendary hunger haunted him like the hound of heaven, and it became, in time, synonymous with life itself. *Appetite.* Slabs of raw life were reduced to crates of raw manuscript. The figure of Wolfe, a piece of manuscript in hand, standing beside a bulging crate of typewritten paper, convincingly symbolizes our raw-material myth and attests to our belief in it. Both the size of the man and the size of the crate are in *scale*.

No greater paradox could be imagined than this raw young giant, a glutton for life, whose experience, in substance, was essentially vicarious. He got it from books. He gives it back to us in books. His lyrical rhetoric and his sober narration—the full range, that is, of his style—derives from his reading, and his reading, like his living, was something he bolted.

"The Function of Appetite," from *The Territory Ahead*, by Wright Morris (New York: Harcourt, Brace and World, 1958), pp. 147–55. Reprinted by permission of the author.

If literature is your life—the artist's life—it, too, must be processed by your imagination. It must be transformed, as raw material is transformed, before it is possessed. In this transformation there is a destructive element. The artist must destroy, in this act of possession, a part of what he loves. In passing it on, through his own achievement, he leaves it different from what he found. It is the element of difference, not sameness, that testifies to his right of possession. But it is the element of sameness—transference rather than transformation—that we find in Wolfe. Described as the Walt Whitman of novelists, here is what he does, how he echoes Whitman:

> Oh, there are women in the East—and new lands, morning, and a shining city! There are forgotten fume-flaws of bright smoke above Manhattan, the forest of masts about the crowded isle, the proud cleavages of departing ships, the soaring web, the wing-like swoop and joy of the great bridge, and men with derby hats who come across the bridge to greet us—come brothers, let us go to find them all. For the huge murmur of the city's million-footed life, far, bee-like, drowsy, strange as time, has come to haunt our ears with all its golden prophecy of joy and triumph, fortune, happiness, and love such as no men before have ever known. Oh brothers . . .

This is meant to be an invocation. What we have is a man with his eyes closed, his pores open, whipping himself into a state of intoxication with what is left of *another* man's observations. The rhetorical flow, lyrical in intent, is unable to keep up with the flow of the emotion, the verbal surge of clichés, of scenic props, to the winded anticlimax of

> the men with derby hats who come across the bridge to greet us—come brothers, let us go to find them all.

The pathetic irrelevance of this touch is central to the flow of fantasy. Rather than Whitman's artifacts, closely and lovingly observed, we have a river of clichés, nouns and soaring adjectives. This giant from the hills may be in love with life, but he woos her with books. It is through another man's eyes that he looks, and it is another man's language that he uses. Life might well ask him, as Priscilla did John Alden, to speak for himself. The presence of raw material, real, raw, bleeding life—the one thing that Wolfe believed he got his big hands on—is precisely what is absent from his work. He begins and he ends with raw-material clichés.

> O youth, still wounded, living, feeling with a woe unutterable, still grieving with a grief intolerable, still thirsting with a thirst unquench-able—where are we to seek? For the wild tempest breaks above us. The wild fury beats about us, the wild hunger feeds upon us—and we are houseless, doorless, unassuaged, and drive on forever: and our brains are mad, our hearts are wild and worldless, and we cannot speak.

This romantic agony, to put it charitably, is strictly literary. He is choking on words in this passage, not on raw life. In a letter to Fitzgerald—frequently cited to show Wolfe's superior vitality and passion—Wolfe made this confession:

> . . . one of my besetting sins, whether you know it or not, is lack of confidence in what I do.

It was a sound intuition. He *knew*, but he did not know *what* he knew. It was a *feeling* he had, but like all of his feelings it remained unexamined, one of his frequent apprehensions, his premonitions of disorder and early sorrow that increased, rather than calmed, his romantic agony. In his effort to both release, and control his muse, he had two styles. Samples of his "release," usually referred to as lyrical flights, I have quoted. In contrast to the lyrical flight is sober, dispassionate, narrative.

> It would have been evident to an observer that of the four people who were standing together at one end of the platform three—the two women and the boy—were connected by the relationship of blood.

This is "control." It is also unintentional parody. Max Beerbohm might have coined it to take care of the great *traditional* novel. Wolfe assumes the stance, he clears his throat, but the voice that issues from his mouth is not his own, and the words fall into unconscious parody. The shades of Thackeray and Trollope, in this prose, were not connected by the relationship of blood.

Periodically, as if purging ourselves of what we spend our lives making and doing, the American mind indulges in a hay ride—one climaxed with a bonfire and love among the haystacks—in order to remind ourselves that there is nobody like us. And indeed there is not. But we are insecure, as Wolfe was insecure, and never tire of the

convincing reminder. The latest, but certainly not the last, was
Thomas Wolfe. He came from the hills. He was six foot four and a
man in every inch. He believed in doing nothing—as Faulkner re-
minds us—short of the impossible. The existence of the legend of
Paul Bunyan may have given young Tom Wolfe something to shoot
at, but in many ways he overshot the mark. The word prodigious—
in energy, in scale, in talent, in ambition, and in failure—is the
word that most happily characterizes the pilgrimage. For Wolfe
made one. He made one for all of us. Although his song is a song of
himself—a choric forest murmur to the lyric Walt Whitman—his
hunger, insatiable as it was, was still too small. It is the continent itself that seeks to speak in the bellow of Wolfe. Everything observ-
able, desirable, and, on certain rare occasions, even conceivable is
thrown into the hopper of his hunger and—*bolted*. Nothing, absolutely *nothing*, is left on the table. We see only where his elbows
leaned, and the crumbs he dropped.

What we observe in Wolfe—if we care to observe him—is how
a man *eats*. As we watch him eat his very appetite grows; he bolts
his food, he reaches for more, and in the very act of gorging himself
he starves to death. It is a vivid and appalling projection of our
buried life. We want to grasp life whole, grasp it raw and bleeding,
and then gulp it while it's hot. Sometimes we do. But the results are
not what we were led to expect. Our appetite, rather than being diminished, has increased. In living out this dream of our buried lives
—in living it up, as we would now describe it—Wolfe threw himself
into the bonfire all of us had built. His identification with the myth,
with its attendant exaltations, and, as the fire began to die, with the
usual premonitions, took on the nature of a public purge and sac-
rifice. These premonitions of death are self-induced; an infinite craving finds its resolution in a craving for the infinite. In his prodigious
effort, in his prodigious failure, was our success. The prevailing
tendency to start well, hewing a path, single-handed, through the
wilderness around him, and then to fail, since to succeed is unheard
of, is a credit to everyone. The highest honors, however, to Wolfe,
the highest praise for his thinking that he could do it—but even
higher honors to the unconquerable continent itself, to us, that is.
We are simply too colossal, as Wolfe was too colossal himself.

When Thomas Wolfe died, at thirty-seven, it was said that had he lived he might have done it, might have grasped what still seemed to elude him, might have tamed the untamable, and in holding out such infinite hope for him, we hold it out for ourselves. It is the sentiment that both sustained and destroyed him—infinite hope, infinite yearning, infinite love, ambition, and hunger, into which the finite world of experience slowly dissolved. An infinite amount of nonraw material overwhelms a very finite fragment of craft, and his barbaric yawp drowned out every voice in the air but his own.

The continent too big for one man to tame it, the story too big for one man to tell it, the manuscript too big for one crate to hold it, one man to shape it—this myth of too-muchness received its classic affirmation in the figure of Wolfe. In identifying himself, lavishly, with the malady that masquerades as a virtue, he lived to the hilt the illusion that is fatal to both the man and the artist. The impotence of *material,* raw or otherwise, receives its widest advertising in his mammoth showcase—almost everything is there but the imagined thing, and all of it bigger than life. The sight of all these objects generated in Wolfe sentiments and sensations of a literary nature, and on occasion, unknowingly, he was moved to something like creative activity. But *that* sensation, singularly unfamiliar, and smacking unmistakably of *self*-control, and self-denial, was the one sensation that he deeply distrusted, distrusted intuitively one might say. That sort of thing led him away from *himself,* and where, if anywhere, did that lead?

He didn't know, and he put off, deliberately, every chance to find out. His artistic solution was to write the same book over and over again, each time in the hope that this time the spirit would inhabit it, each time in the hope that his chronic self-doubt would stop tormenting him. The chorus of praise, world-wide, did not console or beguile him. After all, he *knew.* He knew better than those who hailed his failure as a success. As a martyr to our greed, our insatiable lust for life, which makes life itself an anticlimax, Wolfe is such proof as we need that appetite and raw material are not enough. They are where art begins, but to begin at all calls for the tools of technique.

Loneliness, as a theme of adolescence, rather than aloneness, a condition of man, is what the reader finds in Wolfe and what will assure his continued popularity. It is idle to speak of Wolfe's defects as a writer, since it is precisely the defects that we find immortal. In them, on a cineramic scale, we see ourselves. Wolfe's impressive powers of description persuaded him, as it does most of his readers, that imaginative power of an impressive range was being exercised. On the evidence the contrary is the case, description takes the place of imagination, and an excess of description, a rhetoric of hyperbole, take the place of imaginative passion.

His book—for it is all one book—offers us the extraordinary spectacle, both haunting and appalling, of the artist as a cannibal. An insatiable hunger, like an insatiable desire, is not the sign of life, but of impotence. Impotence, indeed, is part of the romantic agony. If one desires what one cannot have, if one must do what cannot be done, the agony in the garden is one of self-induced impotence. It is Wolfe's tragic distinction to have suffered his agony for us all.

# The Shade of Thomas Wolfe

## by *William Styron*

The shade of Thomas Wolfe must be acutely disturbed to find that his earthly stock has sunk so low. All artists want fame, glory, immortality, yet few were so frankly bent on these things as Wolfe was, and no writer—despite his agonizing self-doubts—seemed so confident that they lay within his grasp. The unabashed desire for perpetuity moves in a rhythmic, reappearing theme through all of his works. In a typically boisterous apostrophe to the power of booze in *Of Time and the River* he chants: "You came to us with music, poetry, and wild joy when we were twenty, when we reeled home at night through the old moon-whitened streets of Boston and heard our friend, our comrade, and our dead companion, shout through the silence of the moonwhite square: 'You are a poet and the world is yours.' . . . We turned our eyes then to the moon-drunk skies of Boston, knowing only that we were young, and drunk, and twenty, and that the power of mighty poetry was within us, and the glory of the great earth lay before us—because we were young and drunk and twenty, and could never die!" But poor Tom Wolfe if not dead is presently moribund and the matter of his resuscitation is certainly in doubt. The young, one is told, being gland- and eyeball-oriented, read very little of anything any more, and if they do it is likely to be Burroughs or Becket or Genet or a few of the bards of black humor or camp pornography. Of the older writers, Hemingway and Fitzgerald are still read, but Wolfe seldom. When the literary temper of a generation is occult, claustrophobic, doom-ridden, and the quali-

"The Shade of Thomas Wolfe," by William Styron. From *Harper's* ccxxxvi (April 1968), pp. 96, 98–102, 104. Reprinted by permission of the author and The Harold Matson Company, Inc.

This essay was written as a review of *Thomas Wolfe: A Biography*, by Andrew Turnbull (New York: Charles Scribner's Sons, 1968).

fied snigger is its characteristic psychic response, no writer could
be so queer as the shambling, celebratory hulk of Thomas Wolfe,
with his square's tragic sense and his bedazzled young man's vision of
the glory of the world. What a comedown! In Europe, with the possible exception of Germany, he is not very well known. No, the reputation of Wolfe is in very bad shape; I suppose it was inevitable that,
a short time ago, when I asked a college English major what he
thought of the work of Thomas (not Tom) Wolfe he actually *did*
reply seriously, "You mean the Tangerine Streamlined Whatever-
it's-called guy?"

Yet it would be hard to exaggerate the overwhelming effect that
reading Wolfe had upon so many of us who were coming of age during or just after the second world war. I think his influence may have
been especially powerful upon those who, like myself, had been
reared as Wolfe had in a small Southern town or city, and who in
addition had suffered a rather mediocre secondary education, with
scant reading of any kind. To a boy who had read only a bad transla-
tion of *Les Misérables* and *The Call of the Wild* and *Men Against
the Sea* and *The Grapes of Wrath* (which one had read at fourteen
for the racy dialogue and the "sensational" episodes), the sudden exposure to a book like *Look Homeward, Angel,* with its lyrical torrent
and raw, ingenuous feeling, its precise and often exquisite rendition
of place and mood, its buoyant humor and the vitality of its characters and, above all, the sense of youthful ache and promise and hunger and ecstasy which so corresponded to that of its eighteen-year-old
reader—to experience such a book as this, at exactly the right moment in time and space, was for many young people like being born
again into a world as fresh and wondrous as that seen through the
eyes of Adam. Needless to say, youth itself was largely responsible for
this feverish empathy, and there will be reservations in a moment in
regard to the effect of a later rereading of Wolfe; nonetheless, a man
who can elicit such reactions from a reader at whatever age is a force
to be reckoned with, so I feel nothing but a kind of gratitude when
I consider how I succumbed to the rough unchanneled force of
Wolfe as one does to the ocean waves.

Among other things, he was the first prose writer to bring a sense
of America as a glorious abstraction—a vast and brooding continent
whose untold bounties were waiting every young man's discovery—

and his endless catalogues and lyric invocations of the land's physical sights and sounds and splendors (a sumptuous description of the Boston waterfront, for instance, where "the delicate and subtle air of spring touches all these odors with a new and delicious vitality; it draws the tar out of the pavements also, and it draws slowly, subtly, from ancient warehouses, the compacted perfumes of eighty years: the sweet thin piney scents of packing boxes, the glutinous composts of half a century, that have thickly stained old warehouse plankings, the smells of twine, tar, turpentine and hemp, and of thick molasses, ginseng, pungent vines and roots and old piled sacking . . . and particularly the smell of meat, of frozen beeves, slick porks, and veals, of brains and livers and kidneys, of haunch, paunch and jowl . . .") seemed to me anything but prolix or tedious, far from it; rather it was as if for the first time my whole being had been thrown open to the sheer *tactile* and *sensory* vividness of the American scene through which, until then, I had been walking numb and blind, and it caused me a thrill of discovery that was quite unutterable. It mattered little to me that sometimes Wolfe went on for page after windy page about nothing, or with the most callow of emotions: I was callow myself, and was undaunted by even his most inane repetitions. It meant nothing to me that some astonishingly exact and poignant rendition of a mood or remembrance might be followed by a thick suet of nearly impenetrable digressions; I gobbled it all up, forsaking my classes, hurting my eyes, and digesting the entire large Wolfe *oeuvre*—the four massive novels, plus the short stories and novellas, *The Story of a Novel,* the many letters and scraps and fragments, and the several plays, even then practically unreadable—in something less than two weeks, emerging from the incredible encounter pounds lighter, and with a buoyant serenity of one whose life has been forever altered.

I think it must have been at approximately this moment that I resolved myself to become a writer. I was at college in North Carolina at the time; it was October, Wolfe's natal, favorite, most passionately remembered month, and the brisk autumnal air was now touched, for the first time in *my* life, with the very fragrance and the light that Wolfe's grand hymn to the season had evoked: "October has come again—has come again. . . . The ripe, the golden month has come again, and in Virginia the chinkapins are falling. Frost sharps the middle music of the seasons, and all things living on the earth turn home again . . . The bee bores to the belly of the yellowed grape, the fly gets old and fat and blue, he buzzes loud, crawls slow, creeps heavily to death, the sun goes down in blood and pollen across the bronzed and mown fields of old October . . . Come to us, Father, while the winds howl in the darkness, for October has come again bringing with it huge prophecies of death and life and the great cargo of the men who will return . . ." With words like this still vivid in my brain, I gazed at the transmuted tobacco-hazed streets of Durham, quite beside myself with wonder, and only the appearance of a sudden, unseasonable snowstorm frustrated my immediate departure—together with a friend, similarly smitten—for Asheville, over two hundred miles away, where we had intended to place flowers on the writer's grave.

Now thirty years after Wolfe's death, the appearance of Andrew Turnbull's biography marks an excellent occasion to try to put the man and his work in perspective. Turnbull's work is a first-rate study, and not the least of its many worthy qualities is its sense of proportion. Too many biographies—especially of literary figures—tend to be overly fleshed-out and are cursed with logorrhea, so that the illustrious subject himself becomes obliterated behind a shower of menus, train tickets, opera programs, itineraries and dull mash notes from lovelorn girls. I could have done without so many of the last item in this present volume—from Wolfe's paramour Aline Bernstein who, though by no means a girl, often fell to gushing at inordinate length; but this is a small complaint since throughout the book Turnbull generally maintains a congenial pace and supplies us with just the proper amount of detail. One of the surprises of the biography is the way in which it manages to be fresh and informative about a person who was probably the most narrowly autobiographical writer who ever lived. The very idea of a life of Thomas Wolfe is enough to invoke dismay if not gentle ridicule since our first reaction is, "But why? Everything he did and saw is in his books." Yet Turnbull, clearly with some calculation, has expertly uncovered certain facts having to do with Wolfe's life which, if not really crucial, are fascinating just *because* we realize that we did not know them before. The actual financial situation of Wolfe's family in Asheville, for example, is interesting since the impression one gets of the deafening tribe of Gants in *Look Homeward, Angel* is that of a down-at-the-heel, lower-middle-class clan which may not have been destitute but which always had a hard time of it making ends meet. The truth of the matter, as Turnbull points out, is that by Asheville standards the Wolfes were literally affluent, belonging to the "top two percent economically." Likewise it turns out that Wolfe had a touch of the sybarite in him; as an instructor at New York University he chose to live by himself in lodgings that for the time must have been very expensive, rather than to share quarters with several others as practically all of the instructors did. Such details would be of little interest, of course, were they not at variance with the portraits of Eugene Gant-George Webber, whose careers in the novels are considerably more penurious, egalitarian, and grubby.

Wolfe was an exasperating man, a warm companion with a rich sense of humor and touching generosity of spirit and, alternately, a bastard of truly monumental dimensions, and it is a tribute to the detachment with which Mr. Turnbull has fashioned his biography that the good Wolfe and the bad Wolfe, seen upon separate occasions, begin to blend together so that what emerges (as in the best of biographies) is a man—in this case a man more complex and driven even than is usual among those of his calling: obsessively solitary yet craving companionship, proud and aloof but at the same time almost childishly dependent, open-handed yet suspicious, arrogant, sweet-hearted, hypersensitive, swinishly callous, gentle—every writer, that is, but magnified. In his mid-twenties, on board a ship returning from Europe, Wolfe met and fell in love with Aline Bernstein, a rich and well-known New York stage designer who was eighteen years older than he was. In the ensuing affair, which was bizarre and tumultuous to say the least, Mrs. Bernstein quite clearly represented a mother-figure, an image of the Eliza Gant from whom, in his first two novels, Tom-Eugene is constantly fleeing as from a Fury, and, with cyclic regularity, returning home to in helpless and sullen devotion. (Julia Wolfe nursed her son until he was three-and-a-half and cut off Tom's beautiful ringlets at nine only after he had picked up lice from a neighbor. How Wolfe escaped being a homosexual is a mystery, but no one has ever made that charge.) The same ambivalent feelings he had toward his mother he expressed in his relations with Aline who though extremely pretentious and rather silly did not deserve the treatment she suffered at his hands, which was largely abominable. He was of course capable of great tenderness and it is obvious that they had many happy moments together, but one cannot help feeling anything but rue for the plight of the poor woman, who had to be subjected to interminable grillings by him about her former lovers and who, when circumstances forced them apart, still was made to endure a barrage of letters in which in the most irrational and cruel terms he accused her of betrayal and un-faithfulness. He also shouted at her that she smelled like goose grease, adding the attractive observation that "all Jews smell like goose grease." It was a hopeless situation and although it makes for grim reading the section on Wolfe's stormy time with Aline is one of the most illuminating in the book, revealing as it does so much of the man'e puerile inability to form any real attachment to anyone, especially a woman—a shallowness of emotional response, on a cer-tain level at least, which caused him to be in perpetual flight and which may be a key to both his failings and his strengths as a writer.

There was also, naturally, his editor Maxwell Perkins—still one more relationship filled with *Sturm und Drang* and, on the part of Wolfe, impositions and demands on another's time and energy so total as to be positively hair-raising. Obviously Perkins was a very fine gentleman, but that a broad streak of masochism ran through his nature there can also be no doubt; only a man born to enjoy ter-rible suffering could have absorbed the pure fact of daily, committed *involvement* which Wolfe's tyrannically dependent personality im-posed. It was of course untrue, as had been hinted during Wolfe's years at Scribner's, that Perkins *wrote* any part of Wolfe's books but certainly he was instrumental in putting them together—maybe not quite as instrumental as Bernard DeVoto implied in his famous re-view of *The Story of a Novel* but a thoroughly dominating force nonetheless. There is no other way that we can interpret the hilari-ous statement which Turnbull—perhaps with irony, perhaps not —makes in a section on the finishing of *Of Time and the River*: "Early in December Perkins summoned Wolfe to his office and told him the book was done. Wolfe was amazed." Yet if it is true that Wolfe wrote the words of the books and if it is also true, as someone said, that the trouble with Wolfe was that he put all of his gigantic struggle into his *work* and not his *art*—a nice distinction—it does look as if DeVoto might not have been too far off the mark after all in asserting that Perkins caused much of the "art" that exists in the sprawling work of Thomas Wolfe. Which is to say a semblance, at least, of form. And it is the lack too often of an organic form—a form arising from the same drives and tensions that inspired the work in the beginning—which now appears to be one of Wolfe's largest failings and is the one that most seriously threatens to undermine his stature as a major writer. The awful contradiction in his books between this formlessness and those tremendous moments which still seem so touched with grandeur as to be imperishable, is unsettling beyond words.

Rereading Wolfe is like visiting again a cherished landscape or town of bygone years where one is simultaneously moved that much could remain so appealingly the same and wonderstruck that one could ever have thought that such-and-such a corner or this or that view had any charm at all. It is not really that Wolfe is dated (I mean the fact of being dated as having to do with basically insincere postures and attitudes: already a lot of Hemingway is dated in a way Wolfe could never be); it is rather that when we now begin to realize how unpulled-together Wolfe's work really is—that same shapelessness that mattered so little to us when we were younger— and how this shapelessness causes or at least allows for a lack of inner dramatic tension without which no writer, not even Proust, can engage our mature attention for long, we see that he is simply telling us, often rather badly, things we no longer care about knowing or need to know. So much that once seemed grand and authoritative now comes off as merely obtrusive, strenuously willed, and superfluous. Which of course makes it all the more disturbing that in the midst of this chaotically verbose and sprawling world there stand out here and there truly remarkable edifices of imaginative cohesion.

Wolfe's first novel, *Look Homeward, Angel,* withstands the rigors of time most successfully and remains his best book, taken as a whole. Here the powers of mind and heart most smoothly find their confluence, while a sense of place (mainly Altamont, or Asheville) and time (a boy's life between infancy and the beginning of adulthood) lend to the book a genuine unity that Wolfe never recaptured in his later works. Flaws now appear, however. A recent rereading

of the book caused me to wince from time to time in a way that I
cannot recall having done during my first reading at eighteen. Wolfe
at that point was deeply under the power of Joyce (whom Wolfe,
incidentally, encountered years later on a tour of Belgium, Turnbull
relates in an engaging episode, but who so awed him that he was
afraid to speak to the great Irishman) and if the influence of *Ulysses*
can be discerned in the book's many strengths it can also be seen in
its gaucheries. An otherwise vivid passage like the following, for example (and there are many such in the book), is diminished rather
than reinforced by the culminating Joyce-like allusion:

> Colonel Pettigrew was wrapped to his waist in a heavy rug, his
> shoulders were covered with a gray Confederate cape. He bent forward,
> leaning his old weight upon a heavy polished stick, which his freckled
> hands gripped upon the silver knob. Muttering, his proud powerful
> old head turned shakily from side to side, darting fierce splintered
> glances at the drifting crowd. He was a very parfit gentil knight.

But *Look Homeward, Angel* can be forgiven such lapses precisely because it is a youthful book, as impressive for its sheer lyri-
cism and hymnal celebration of youth and life as is the Mendelssohn
*Violin Concerto,* from which we do not expect profundities, either.
In addition, the novel is quite extraordinarily *alive*—alive in the vitality of its words (Wolfe wrote many bad sentences but *never* a
dead one), in its splendid evocation of small-town sights and sounds
and smells and, above all and most importantly, in the characters
that spring out fully fleshed and breathing from the pages. The figures of W. O. and Eliza Gant are as infuriatingly garrulous and
convincing now as when I first made their acquaintance, and the
death of the tragic older brother Ben is fully as moving for the simple reason that Wolfe has made me believe in his existence. With all
of its topheaviness and the juvenile extravagances that occasionally
mar the surface of the narrative, *Look Homeward, Angel* seems likely
to stand as long as any novel will as a record of early twentieth-century provincial American life.

It is when we run into *Of Time and the River* and its elephantine
successors, *The Web and the Rock* and *You Can't Go Home Again,*
that the real trouble begins. One of the crucial struggles that any
writer of significance has had to endure is his involvement in the

search for a meaningful theme, and Wolfe was no exception. The evidence is that Wolfe, though superbly gifted at imaginative projection, was practically incapable of extended dramatic invention, his creative process being akin to the setting into motion of some marvelous mnemonic tape recorder deep within his cerebrum, from which he unspooled reel after reel of the murmurous, living past. Such a technique served him beautifully in *Look Homeward, Angel,* unified as it was in time and space and from both of which it derived its dramatic tension; but in the later works as Tom-Eugene-George moved into other environments—the ambience of Harvard and New York and, later, of Europe—the theme which at first had been so fresh and compelling lost its wings and the narrator became a solipsistic groundling. Certainly the last three books are still well worth reading; there is still the powerful, inexorable rush of language, a Niagara of words astonishing simply by virtue of its primal energy; many of the great set pieces hold up with their original force: old Gant's death, the *Oktoberfest* sequence in Munich, the apartment-house fire in New York, the portraits of Eugene's Uncle Bascom, Foxhall Edwards, the drunken Dr. McGuire—there are many more. These scenes and characterizations would alone guarantee Wolfe a kind of permanence, even if one must sift through a lot of detritus to find them. But there is so much now that palls and irritates. That furrow-browed, earnest sense of discovery in which the reader participates willingly in *Look Homeward, Angel* loses a great deal of its vivacity when the same protagonist has begun to pass into adulthood. In *Of Time and the River,* for example, when Eugene has become a student at Harvard, we are introduced to a young student named Francis Starwick:

> He spoke in a strange and rather disturbing tone, the pitch and timbre of which it would be almost impossible to define, but which would haunt one who had heard it forever after. His voice was neither very high nor low, it was a man's voice and yet one felt it might also have been a woman's; but there was nothing at all effeminate about it. It was simply a strange voice compared to most American voices, which are rasping, nasal, brutally coarse or metallic. Starwick's voice had a disturbing lurking resonance, an exotic, sensuous and almost voluptuous quality. Moreover, the peculiar mannered affectation of his speech was so studied that it hardly escaped extravagance. If it had not been

for the dignity, grace and intelligence of his person, the affectation of his speech might have been ridiculous. As it was, the other youth felt the moment's swift resentment and hostility that is instinctive with the American when he thinks someone is speaking in an affected manner.

In the first place, his voice wouldn't "haunt one who had heard it forever after." This exaggerated sensibility, this club-footed gawky boy's style, becomes increasingly apparent throughout all of Wolfe's later work, in which the author-protagonist, now out in the world of Northern sophisticates, falls unconsciously into the role of the suspicious young hick from Buncombe County, North Carolina. In the passage just quoted the reader, Starwick—indeed everyone but Eugene Gant—is aware that Starwick is a homosexual, but these labored and sophomoric observations have so begun to dominate Wolfe's point of view that much later on in the book, when Starwick's homosexuality *is* revealed, Eugene's chagrin over that belated knowledge fills the reader with murderous exasperation. The same passage illustrates another trait which crops up increasingly in the later books, and that is a tendency to generalize promiscuously about places and things which demand, if anything, narrow and delicate particularization—especially about a place as various and as chaotically complex as America. The part about voices, for instance. Most American voices, though sometimes unpleasant, are not generally "rasping, nasal, brutally coarse or metallic"; forty or fifty million soft Southern voices alone, including presumably Wolfe's, are—whatever else—the antithesis of all those careless adjectives. Nor is it at all accurate to proclaim either that "the American"—presumably meaning all Americans—feels resentment and hostility at affected speech or that the reaction is peculiarly American. Many Americans are simply tickled or amused by such speech, while at the same time it is surely true that if resentment and hostility are felt, they can be felt by the French over French affectations as well. Wolfe's writing is filled with such silly hyperbole. Similarly a statement such as "we are so lost, so naked, and so lonely in America"— a refrain that reappears over and over again in Wolfe's work—seems to me the worst sort of empty rant, all the more so because Wolfe himself surely knew better, knew that lostness, nakedness, loneliness are not American but part of the whole human condition.

It is sad that so much disappoints on a rereading of Wolfe, sad that the "magic and the singing and the gold" which he celebrated so passionately seem now, within his multitudinous pages, to possess a lackluster quality to which the middle-aging heart can no longer respond. It is especially sad because we can now see (possibly because of the very contrast with all that is so prolix and adolescent and unfelt and labored) that at his best Wolfe was capable of those epiphanies that only writers of a very high order have ever achieved. . . .

Wolfe would have to be cherished if only for the power he exerted upon a whole generation. But even if this were not enough, the clear glimpses he had at certain moments of man as a strange, suffering animal alone beneath the blazing and indifferent stars would suffice to earn him honor, and a flawed but undeniable greatness.

# Thomas Wolfe and the Kicking Season

## by *Pamela Hansford Johnson*

To nearly every successful and serious writer, either during his lifetime or within a short period after it, there comes the Kicking Season. This is not arranged or concerted by villains in committee; it just happens because something is abroad in the air, a sense that it is high time somebody got his come-uppance, was "reappraised," or simply, in his own best interests, given a temporary check. I remember it happening to Hemingway when *Across the River and Into the Trees* came out. I detected a faint whiff of it—very faint— over Mr. Eliot's last play. The higher they rise. . . . Yes, one day it will even be the turn of Scott Fitzgerald. Even of Mr. E. M. Forster. At the moment, it is the turn of poor Tom Wolfe.

"This man is not a novelist," wrote Mr. Cyril Connolly, on September 14th last, when a new edition of *Look Homeward, Angel* and Wolfe's *Selected Letters* were issued together, "he is an obsessional neurotic with a gift for words who could write only about himself and who cannot create other people. He is the Benjamin Robert Haydon of American literature." The late Edwin Muir headed his article, "The Pretender," and wrote, "His novels have become almost unreadable," quoting, to prove it, a good deal of Wolfe's old nonsense and little of his excellence. In the whole of *Look Homeward Angel* he found only one convincing character, "Elizabeth Gant." It is odd to see her as Elizabeth. She was Eliza to us.

"Thomas Wolfe and the Kicking Season," by Pamela Hansford Johnson. From *Encounter*, xii, April 1959), pp. 87–90. Copyright © Pamela Hansford Johnson. Reprinted by permission of the author.

This essay was written as a review of *Look Homeward, Angel* (Heinemann), and *Selected Letters of Thomas Wolfe,* edited, with an Introduction by Elizabeth Nowell.

By "us," I mean a group of young men and girls at the beginning of the 'thirties, either just within or just out of their teens, reared in a London suburb, good grammar school products, liking to roll back the carpet in the evenings and dance, and to flow through successive crazes for successive writers. What writers? Well, there was a long run on Dostoievsky; on O'Flaherty: a short but (for me) painful one on Nietzsche: and then, one day, *Look Homeward Angel* burst upon us like the radiance from a lighthouse newly erected upon some very sticky rocks. We ate, drank, and dreamed it. We weren't fools. We had some taste, we knew that some of it was guff. The apostrophes of Eugene to Ann, that "great big beautiful Boston bitch," made us wriggle. But that book spoke for us: spoke, not in spite of its sprawlings, its bawlings, its youthful yellings and howlings about the family, the silver cord, the "incommunicable prison of this earth," love itself, but because of those things, We were not articulate ourselves, though we had much we wanted to say. Wolf had far too much to say, but he said it with our voices.

In the *Manchester Guardian* of October 3rd last, Mrs. Doris Lessing, that soberly diagnostic critic, wrote with her usual sense, her usual lack of flummery, that Wolfe was a myth-maker: "He did not write *about* adolescence: to read him is to re-experience adolescence. . . . I have yet to meet a person born into any kind of Establishment who understood Wolfe, I have yet to meet a provincial who has cracked open a big city who does not acknowledge that Wolfe expressed his own struggle for escape into larger experience."

And there you have it, pat: "the *whole* thing," as Starwick would have said.

For it is no good denying one's enthusiasm, once they have been excited. There must have been something to back them, in proportion to their violence. These boys and girls I have spoken of didn't even mind the rhetoric—"O lost, and by the wind grieved, ghost, come back again . . ."—and it was encouraging to me to find a positive response to this threnody by an otherwise stern young man in *Granta,* at the end of last year. So he should respond, unless he were dead already. We did. We couldn't help it.

*The Times Literary Supplement,* in an excellent middle article, paid Wolfe the tribute of taking him seriously, and praising where praise was due. This mentioned his "gift of mimicry" (first-class, by the way), and his masterly ability to transfer the flavour of a person to the printed page. The writer also, and this was salutary, reminded us of Faulkner's almost wildly generous praise of Wolfe. He "put Wolfe first" among his contemporaries: "We all fail, but Wolfe made the best failure because he tried hardest to say the most." Mr. Faulkner is not an ass. He would not have been so carried away by a writer who was an ass—utterly.

Because the assish side of Wolfe is indisputable, and the *Selected Letters* make it worse. Such Pecksniffery! (Though we should have guessed it from Eugene's absurd farewell to Starwick in *Of Time and the River*.) So many gentle, mellifluous, seeping openings, full of love, to letters that degenerate into sadic abuse. All the worst of Wolfe is in his letter to some poor girl brought along to him at Harvard, whom he found somewhat loose; in his letter to the "Ann" of *Of Time and the River*, mulling over the Ann-Eleanor-Starwick rumpus in Paris; in the disgraceful letter refusing to allow *I Have a Thing to Tell You* to be translated into Yiddish, on the grounds that it wasn't really political at all and he couldn't have it used to political ends. All the best of Wolfe is in the letters of travel, in particular the letter about Hungary which he wrote to Aline Bernstein.

A surprising number of contemporary critics approve the letters and reject the novel. This I fail to understand. The same man wrote both. Out of the stuff, both splendid and repulsive, of these letters, came the novels. I am, of course, biased. In 1947 I published a short critical book on Wolfe. I would stand by all in it that is essential: I would like to modify some apologetic passages which apologise for nothing, and certainly explain nothing away. But while I was writing it I was carried along by the Tom Wolfe who meant so much to me when I was young; and now that I am not so young, I can still re-read the best of him and know that the best was pretty good.

Shortly after the book appeared in America I received a fascinating letter from a lady who had known him well. She began: "You must realise that Tom was never the same after he was kicked on the head by a horse."

Owing to a gross mischance, that letter was mislaid somewhere on the premises of the National Book League, and I have lost the address of the writer. There is so much I want to know. What horse? And, perhaps more pertinently, when?

For there was always something kickable, or already kicked, about Wolfe. If it wasn't horses, it was critics. His hugeness of body and intention invited it: and he shrank from the hoof like a sea-anemone from a proffered stone. Poor chap, we all take it hard, but, like Mrs. Gummidge (and there is a great deal of Mrs. Gummidge in Tom) he took it worst.

Wolfe had almost all the virtues of the major novelist except good taste and power of organisation; Good taste, of course, is a virtue easily overrated: Balzac was not conspicuous for it, and remains one of the greatest of all novelists. Organisational power, however, is essential if taste is lacking; and after *Look Homeward Angel* Wolfe gave up any attempt to organise whatsoever. Furthermore, he was not intellectual in the sense that Proust, James, Tolstoy, were. In their sense Dickens, of course, was not, and nor was Balzac: but both were magnificent organisers of their material, and if a writer is to succeed with only a middling intellectual equipment he must be able to organise, or he is up against it.

What Wolfe had, however, was the splendid capacity to lend dignity and marmoreal stature to the fact of being young. Aldous Huxley succeeded by flattering the youth of his day. The young people who loved him were not (they knew) as clever as he; but he held out the hope that if they used their brains hard enough they might one day hope to respond to him on more or less equal terms. He did not speak as one of them: but he never talked down. Wolfe spoke from among them: he was a great, bossy, tormented voice in their crowd. He spoke for them: they cried Hooray. Out of their dumb, secreted music he made a big noisy song.

That was his main contribution to the novel; he was, as Mrs. Lessing says, a myth-maker. In his gigantic person he embodied the entire myth of his time. She observes also:

> He was . . . packed with prejudices. Any thing or person alien to him was an enemy. His attitudes towards Negroes and Jews were crudely instinctual. Some of his ideas about women were juvenile. He hated and loved like a child, according to whether or not he was loved and accepted. He had no notion of politics at all. . . .

It is perfectly true. He was not only an adolescent like us: he was a sillier adolescent. We loved him because he spoke for us and because he was an artist; but we didn't feel the need to look up to him. We had more sense. And we felt the warmer to him because he had less than we.

If the word "artist" has any meaning at all, of course Wolfe was one. He did not know how to order the whole of his vast material, but he did know how to turn a death in the family, a humiliation in love, into art. I cannot conceive how anyone can read of the death of Ben Gant, the episodes with Abe Jones at N.Y.U., the nightmare quartet in Paris, Eugene, Eleanor, Ann, and Starwick, the first excitement of prowling the book-stacks at Harvard, without accepting the fact. I wrote in my own book: "There are three deaths in literature comparable for power and pity and horror with the death of Ben: the death of Oliver Gant, in *Of Time and the River,* of the father in Roger Martin du Gard's *Les Thibault,* and of the grandmother in *A la Recherche du Temps Perdu.* The nervous strain of it, the appalling grief, and above all the pervasive *bad temper* are suggested with an extraordinary nakedness and force."

I don't feel like going back on that. The scene is wonderful because it is autobiography, because it is personally felt: but art has arranged it. After all, the majority of mankind manage to feel. Only a small number can convey their emotions to others.

The trouble with Wolfe now is that he runs counter to anything we have learned recently to respect. He is pre-eminently Bad Form—or would be if he had a form. He is politically reprehensible—or would be if he had any coherent politics. He throws up bizarre additional difficulties by his hidden ambivalence. In *Look Homeward Angel* we have the romanticised figure of Laura James, the moonlight-and-roses woven about her. But what is she beside the love-figure of Francis Starwick? And again, what is Starwick's stature in relation to that of Esther Jack, in the last two novels? Greater? or less? How far did Wolfe understand himself? Less, I should say, than a serious novelist must. Yet he was profoundly serious in intention. I believe he had more of the gifts of the great novelist than any American of his century: but failed because his flaws were insufficiently compensated.

We all value the organised intellect. We properly turn from the intellect totally out of control (Frederick Rolfe) and from the control without intellect (no names, no pack-drill). But we find it hard to look at Wolfe straight, or settle our energies to discovering where he was in full control of his artistic material, and what, at best, he made of it. The *Selected Letters,* how ever fine some of them may be, can do him no good. For here is Wolfe screaming and howling at his worse, patronising and sermonising at his worst, biting, at his worst, the hands that fed him. The fact that many of these letters remained unposted is significant enough. Wolfe was sufficiently in control of his material, in the physical sense, not to drop it in the pillar-box. The story of his novels is in them, but it is not the story as he finally wrote it. He chose to write it better.

Are Wolfe's faults finally destructive, denying him a serious position in American literature? There is no doubt they are pretty bad. At his very worst, he makes one blush; but there is much to blush at in Balzac too (only *he* would have put a pirate with a grand piano into a story so psychologically subtle as *Une Femme de Trente Ans*), and not a little in Lawrence: the Natcha-Kee-Tawara tribe in *The Lost Girl* is only just bearable. Is Wolfe's intellectual immaturity intolerable? It is true that as we get older, so we increasingly dislike being shouted at. Can we write him off because we don't know, in *Of Time and the River, The Web and the Rock, You Can't Go Home Again,* how much of such organisation as there is, is due to him, and how much to Maxwell Perkins and Aswell? Can we no longer bear the rhetoric? For my part, I should like to see some return to it in our writing. We have thrown it out entirely have left ourselves the drier and the more brittle. Dickens' rhetoric was not infrequently one of his most vitalising factors, and Proust (*"O grandes attitudes de l'Homme et de la Femme . . . "*) used it like song, when there was a time for song. Perhaps we can no longer bear *Wolfe's* rhetoric? Well, some of it is splendid, and the rest not much worse than better writers have got away with.

I am inclined to think that, so far as he is concerned, this is *merely* a Kicking Season, and not a definite reappraisal. What we shall have to do, eventually, is to sort Wolfe down. We must sort him down in our own minds while we read him, even as we sort Balzac down, accepting the work as a whole (because both the good and the bad make up the whole of any writer), while keeping our own reservations. Wolfe came nearer than any other writer to producing the

"Great American Novel" in its mythopoeic sense. His is a young book risen out of a young culture; it attempts too much, just as he, poor devil, attempted too much when he tried to read all at once all the books ever written. But William Faulkner must still have the last word on him. What he said may have been the overspill of an enormous impulse of generosity: yet he meant it at the time, as we who were young when the 'thirties began meant our enthusiasm at the time. And such praise, such grateful affection, doesn't spring out of nothing. Wolfe, at times, writes like Hell or James Joyce. At others, he writes like a great novelist. How many writers can do as much?

There is somebody else who writes at times like a great novelist, and that is James Hanley. But he has never had a Kicking Season—(*a*) because he has never had a season of assured success, and (*b*) because when *he* writes badly, he doesn't offend the taste, he doesn't raise the blush, he isn't rowdy, he isn't silly: he is just glum and dull. Hanley and Wolfe both have qualities of greatness—very different ones; and wrecking qualities—very different ones. Both have a vast sense of *scale*, both think big. One made a lot of money, one can't have made much. Yet the critical intelligence which can write either off as negligible defeats me. As I have said, I would not apologise for the worst of Wolfe as I apologised for it ten years ago. I do not feel, as Mr. Connolly does, that he would have improved had he lived. I think he would have got much, much worse. In any case, his young death was an essential part of his work: I don't know how he managed to see it coming (*"Something has spoken to me in the night and told me I must die"*) but he did. Such organisational powers as he had were gone. Such intellectual detachment as he had, was gone. His work was left in chaos, he had seen the world as chaos. Romantically Germanophile, only in part disillusioned by Martha Dodd, he could not have faced the new war. He must be judged on what he has left, and no excuses should be made for him. He would have hated them, and would have reacted, I have no doubt, in letters of really appalling Pecksniffery.

"Do not suppose that your kind review, your really *great* review, of my work gave me aught but pleasure. You are too fine a person, I know, too generous a person, to have written out of anything that was not honest and big. . . . If I say that you disgust me, that for a whole night and day I could not bear to turn my eyes to where the magazine lay which contained your 'appraisal,' you will realise that I say it only as a friend, in the hope that you may some day come to realise . . ." etcetera, etcetera.

Something like that.

# Thomas Wolfe: *Look Homeward, Angel*

## *by Thomas C. Moser*

It is difficult to speak of Thomas Wolfe except in extreme terms, in superlatives. Even in his lifetime he was a legend; friends, reviewers, and the public referred to him with Hollywood adjectives—stupendous, gigantic, immense. Clearly Wolfe did think of himself in this way and, in a certain sense, these absurd American words are appropriate. He really was a huge man: six and a half feet tall, weighing about two hundred and fifty pounds at his death in 1938, and he looked even larger. His friends report that he walked in long, aggressive strides and threw his arms about in extravagant gestures. He had a gargantuan appetite, not only because he was so big but because he often took time for only one real meal a day. He was as hungry for experience as for food; he wanted, as he said, to explore life "with an encyclopedic thoroughness." Still a student at Harvard and not yet a novelist, he wrote to his mother:

> I know this now: I am inevitable. I sincerely believe that the only thing that can stop me now is insanity, disease, or death. . . . I will go everywhere and see everything. I will meet all the people I can. I will think all the thoughts, feel all the emotion I am able, and will write, write, write.

Write he did. He proved appallingly that he was not simply a giant sponge, inertly absorbing the world. He often wrote for fifteen hours out of twenty-four. Early one morning in New York City, a friend heard a distant chant and looked out the window:

"Thomas Wolfe: *Look Homeward, Angel*," by Thomas C. Moser. From *The American Novel: From James Fenimore Cooper to William Faulkner*, ed. by Wallace Stegner. © 1965 by Basic Books, Inc., Publishers, New York. Reprinted by permission of the publisher.

There was Tom, in his battered black fedora and long dark-blue rain-coat, swinging along at his tremendous stride and chanting over and over, "I wrote ten thousand words today. I wrote ten thousand words today." [1]

In his hopeless attempt to get everything down on paper, he could not bear to cut out anything:

The business of selection and revision is simply hell for me—my efforts to cut out 50,000 words may sometimes result in my adding 75,000.

When he died, Wolfe had published two very long novels and had left behind a pile of manuscript eight feet high.

But how good was it? *Look Homeward, Angel* has continued to be popular, more popular perhaps than any serious novel by a contemporary. Yet, except for Malcolm Cowley, leading literary critics, most of whom are academics, give it little recognition. But if academics have been cold toward Wolfe, a great writer was not. In 1951, William Faulkner surprisingly ranked Wolfe first among contemporary American writers, himself second, Dos Passos third, and Hemingway fourth. Faulkner explained the ranking this way:

I rated Wolfe first because we had all failed but Wolfe had made the best failure because he had tried the hardest to say the most. . . . My admiration for Wolfe is that he tried his best to get it all said; he was willing to throw away style, coherence, all the rules of preciseness, to try to put all the experience of the human heart on the head of a pin, as it were.[2]

Readers over thirty find Thomas Wolfe difficult to appreciate—not to understand but to appreciate. He often writes very badly, even in *Look Homeward, Angel,* the most finished of his novels. As Faulkner said, Wolfe throws away style and coherence. One recalls that embarrassing passage early in the novel where the infant hero, Eugene Gant, in his crib, thinks of

the discomfort, weakness, dumbness, the infinite misunderstanding he would have to endure. . . . He grew sick as he thought of the weary

---

[1] Nancy Hale, quoted in Elizabeth Nowell, *Thomas Wolfe,* "A Biography" (Garden City, N.Y.: Doubleday, 1960), p. 14.

[2] Quoted in Richard Walser, ed., *The Enigma of Thomas Wolfe* (Cambridge, Mass.: Harvard University Press, 1953), p. vii.

distance before him, the lack of co-ordination of the centres of control, the undisciplined and rowdy bladder, the helpless exhibition he was forced to give in the company of his sniggering, pawing brothers and sisters, dried, cleaned, revolved before them. . . .

He understood that "no one ever comes really to know anyone," that "caught in that insoluble prison of being, we escape it never. . . . Never, never, never, never, never." As he looked at the "huge leering heads that bent hideously into his crib, . . . his brain went black with terror." This passage has been called the "silliest" in serious fiction, not merely because of the gross violation of probability, but because of the sentimentality, the unmotivated hysteria, and, simply, the ineptitude: inserting the five famous "nevers" from *King Lear,* using such a melodramatic cliché as "his brain went black with terror."

Although *Look Homeward, Angel* is his most unified novel, much of the unity is superficial, imposed gratuitously by the subject matter. A middle-class boy, growing up in a small American city, follows an almost predictable series of experiences. Despite Wolfe's frequent assertions of connections, one feels very little sense of growth in the main character, of relations between characters, or of the impact of event upon character. Although the dramatized incidents are often utterly persuasive, even very moving, their effects upon the characters are not realized. Wolfe is a perfect example of Hemingway's famous statement: "You'll lose it if you talk about it." When Eugene argues with his mother, when he loses his girl friend, when his roommate dies—in each case Wolfe talks about the painful effects, and each time he loses much of the feeling created by the dramatized scene. The dialogue and the gestures are just right; the hero's thoughts and the author's comments are often wrong.

Failing so radically in the two crucial artistic requirements of style and coherence, surely Wolfe deserves our indifference. But he does not always fail in these matters, and he succeeds brilliantly in other ways. If we let his weaknesses obscure his strengths, the fault may lie, after all, with ourselves. According to the publisher,

Each new generation as it comes along rediscovers and claims this book for its own. For Wolfe wrote about youth, and he spoke to youth more convincingly than any American writer has ever done.

To appreciate Wolfe older readers must be willing to recall their own youth sympathetically and to look again at the world with youthful eyes—eyes that, despite the distortions of sentimentality, may see in some ways more clearly than those of age.

Why do academic critics disapprove of Wolfe? Partly, at least, because Wolfe did not write the kind of book an American novelist of the 1920's *ought* to have written. Somehow, Wolfe ought to have written in the tradition of Flaubert and James and Conrad, the tradition of exquisite craftsmanship. Hemingway and Fitzgerald are the obvious exemplars. Or, Wolfe should have been an experimenter in technique, like Joyce and Faulkner. Although Wolfe deeply admired Conrad and Joyce, he wrote very old-fashioned novels, a mélange of the picaresque—Fielding, Dickens, Twain—and of the spiritual autobiography—the English romantics, Melville, Whitman.

But if Wolfe's manner is old-fashioned, his matter belongs to our century. When the wisest man in Conrad's *Lord Jim* is asked to diagnose the hero's ailment, he replies: "I understand very well. He is romantic." Conrad's subject, the youthful, romantic egoist, is Wolfe's subject. The hero of *Look Homeward, Angel* has affinities, too, with Fitzgerald's Jay Gatsby and with Faulkner's Quentin Compson in *The Sound and the Fury*. But there is an important difference. These other novelists keep their romantic heroes in check: Conrad and Fitzgerald through a subordinate, ironic narrator; Faulkner through the perspectives of other characters, other points of view. But Thomas Wolfe—Eugene Gant—simply expresses, expresses, expresses his romantic emotions.

> I intend to wreak out my soul on paper and express it all. This is what my life means to me: I am at the mercy of this thing and I will do it or die.

*Look Homeward, Angel* begins with a kind of prose poem:

> . . . a stone, a leaf, an unfound door; of a stone, a leaf, a door.
> . . . we seek the great forgotten language, the lost lane-end into heaven, a stone, a leaf, an unfound door. Where? When?

Like many romantic tales, then, this is the story of a quest, a quest that can never be successfully completed. Just as Gatsby forever pursues the green light, so Eugene Gant's quest finds its symbol in the leaf, stone, and door. Eugene is full of "desire and longing" for some vague perfection never precisely located. As a boy growing up in an isolated provincial town, Eugene often believes his "happy land" lies outside the cup of the mountains, perhaps in the deep South, burning "like Dark Helen in [his] blood," or perhaps in some "golden city." Since the railroad train is his means of escape, train whistles have a special poignancy for him. More frequently, Eugene locates his happy land in the world of imagination, dreams, and artistic creation. He seems to place this in a wonderful cave, entered through an underground passage:

> He groped for the doorless land of faery, that illimitable haunted country that opened somewhere below a leaf or a stone.

Again, Eugene's quest leads toward communication with another person, with his dearest brother, Ben, or with his beloved Laura James. Here, the door leads not to an underground faeryland but rather through the barrier separating personalities. Often, borrowing Wordsworth's notion of a prenatal paradise, Wolfe locates his goal in the past, either in some heaven where he lived before birth or in the actual past of his childhood. Finally, at the very end of the novel, Eugene says that he has found his happy land:

> . . . in the city of myself, upon the continent of my soul, I shall find the forgotten language, the lost world, a door where I may enter.

Self-knowledge, then, appears to be the key to the door. Or rather, the door seems to open upon the individual's inner, buried life.

Although Wolfe asserts that the quest has ended, and although at times Eugene glimpses his goal, the prevailing mood of the hero is frustration. Note that the initial prose poem is less about the quest than about loneliness and loss.

> Which of us has known his brother? Which of us has looked into his father's heart? Which of us has not remained forever prison-pent? Which of us is not forever a stranger and alone? . . . O lost, and by the wind grieved, ghost, come back again.

As a matter of fact, Wolfe's first title for the novel was "O, Lost," and the second, "Alone, Alone." The title he finally chose comes from John Milton's elegy, "Lycidas," in which the poet asks the angel, St. Michael, to look back toward England and melt with pity at the spectacle of a promising young man's death by drowning. While Fitzgerald portrays Gatsby as a young man with an "extraordinary gift for hope," Eugene and Wolfe recognize that utter loneliness is man's lot and that ceaseless change, immutable Time, and Death inevitably frustrate longings for the happy land.

The circumstances of Wolfe's own life make this obsession with change and loss quite comprehensible. One of his earliest memories was the death of his brother Grover, when Wolfe was only four. At six came the wrench of having to leave the warm center of his life, his father's house, for the impersonal, transient chaos of his mother's boardinghouse. Much later he wrote:

> I was without a home—a vagabond since I was seven—with two roofs and no home. . . . I think I learned about being alone when I was a child . . . and I think that I have known about it ever since.

It is hardly surprising that he describes Eugene as "a stranger in a noisy inn." Eugene sees little evidence that anyone else transcends loneliness. He and his brothers and sisters feel only embarrassment when they watch their father's clumsy attempts to embrace their mother: "Aw, Papa, don't." Wolfe used to say that the most tragic event of his life was the death, when he was eighteen, of his favorite bother, Ben. But perhaps even more important was the constant awesome sense of his father's ultimate end, the awareness that the most vital, heroic figure in his life was doomed.

Furthermore, the town in which Wolfe grew up was also undergoing convulsive change. Asheville, North Carolina (Altamont in the novel), is not quite a typical Southern town. Although it underwent the pain of the post-Civil War era, its location high in the Appalachian Mountains gives it a climate that attracted people from the outside world. By the turn of the century, Asheville had become an important health resort and a popular vacation spot. Northern millionaires settled in Asheville, real estate values soared, and the population doubled. Wolfe grew up in an environment that displayed simultaneously Southern defeat and Northern "progress," Southern poverty and Northern materialism. Every year he saw another piece of his cherished past obliterated, until finally his father's tombstone shop gave way to a skyscraper.

Although the themes of loneliness and loss are enormously important to Wolfe, their mere expression does not contribute great significance to the novel. Aching so to be happy and knowing that he cannot, Eugene responds in an adolescent way: he feels sorry for himself. Moreover, the older he becomes the more naked is the self-pity and the less interesting the central character. When Wolfe writes badly, the subject is almost always Eugene.

However, if Wolfe's sense of the inevitability of loss seriously tarnishes the central character of *Look Homeward, Angel,* it also inspires what is truly great in the novel. Conrad defined the writer's task this way:

> To snatch in a moment of courage, from the remorseless rush of time, a passing phase of life.[3]

Just as Wolfe's father carved stone monuments to the dead, so Wolfe memorializes his lost past: the earth at her most opulent, his home town in its variety, and his family in their frenetic activity. The Gant family is, of course, the Wolfe family, even to some of the names. In a court case involving real estate in Asheville, *Look Homeward, Angel* was admitted in testimony as a historical record.

What matters, though, is not where these materials came from, but the way in which Wolfe brings them to life. He said:

> My memory is characterized . . . by the intensity of its sense impressions, its power to evoke and bring back the odors, sounds, colors, shapes, and feel of things with concrete vividness.

To the same degree that Wolfe despairs that everything must pass, he jealously cherishes and celebrates what is most imbued with life. Haunted by Time, he describes the earth best in terms of the passing seasons:

> The plum-tree, black and brittle, rocks stiffly in winter wind. Her million little twigs are frozen in spears of ice. But in the spring, lithe and heavy, she will bend under her great load of fruit and blossoms. She will grow young again. Red plums will ripen, will be shaken desperately upon the tiny stems. They will fall bursted on the loamy warm wet earth; when the wind blows in the orchard the air will be filled with dropping plums; the night will be filled with the sound of their drop-

---

[3] Preface to *The Nigger of the "Narcissus"* (New York: Doubleday, 1936), p. xiv.

ping, and a great tree of birds will sing, burgeoning, blossoming richly,
filling the air also with warm-throated plum-dropping bird-notes.

Whereas poetic accounts of Eugene's loneliness generally contain
Wolfe's worst prose, the lyric evocations of the physical world often
represent Wolfe's best.

Even more than the earth and its plenty, Wolfe wanted to celebrate the people of his homeland, his family especially, but also the
whole range of humanity in the town. Wherever Eugene goes
through the streets of Altamont, he *sees* someone. When he glances
up at the second story window of a dental building, a tiny breeze
blows back the curtains, revealing Dr. H. M. Smathers,

> white-jacketed, competent, drill in hand. He pumped vigorously with
> his right foot, took a wad of cotton from his assistant, Miss Lola Bruce,
> and thrusting it securely into the jaw of his unseen patient, bent his
> fashionable bald head intently. . . . "Do you feel that?" he said ten-
> derly. "Wrogd gdo gurk!" "Spit!"

Though Wolfe can be prolix, he brings to life an array of minor
characters with a few striking details of speech, dress, or gesture
and with a fine gift for comedy. There is the apparently endless
series of predatory, middle-aged females who pass through Eliza's
boardinghouse, "Dixieland," and have affairs with the Gant males,
from W. O. in his sixties to Eugene in his middle teens. In his portraits of the two best doctors in town, Wolfe combines comedy with
deep admiration. We see them not only in their offices but also at
5:30 A.M. before surgery, sitting on stools in the Uneeda Lunch
No. 3: McGuire "patiently impaling kidney beans, one at a time,
upon the prongs of his fork," the odor of corn whiskey soaking the
air about him. "His thick skilful butcher's hands, hairy on the
backs," grip the fork "numbly." He speaks in a "barking kindly
voice." Coker, the Lung Shark, watches "McGuire's bean hunt with
sardonic interest," takes the long cigar out of his "devil's head," and
holds it "between his stained fingers." To Ben Gant's irritated plea
that McGuire not be permitted to operate in such a condition,
Coker responds, "Why, he's just getting hot, son." And the truth is
that these two grotesques are humane, expert healers.

Wolfe's greatest triumph in *Look Homeward, Angel* is, of course,
the re-creation of his own family, the Gants. Although Eugene at

some point hates every member of the family, Wolfe himself loves these creations: "to me . . . they were the greatest people I had ever known. . . . If I could get my magnificent people on paper as they were. . . ." Magnificent they are, and emphatically a *family:* "They had twisted the design of all orderly life, because there was in them a mad, original, disturbing quality." Above all, there is their fantastic energy: they appear to live without need of sleep; they are all compulsive talkers, whether in the slow, deliberate utterances of Eliza, or the idiotic outbursts of Luke, the engineering student: "He was not an electrical engineer—he was electrical energy." In Helen the "hysteria of constant excitement" lurks. Like Eugene, they are all embarked on a quest though, except perhaps for old Gant, none of them seems quite aware of the fact. Helen instinctively gropes "toward a center of life and purpose to which she [can] fasten her energy." Ben, so ironic, disdainful, and independent, tries to get at life by reading the success sermons of millionaires in the *Post*.

Despite their consistent family resemblances, the Gants are all brilliantly defined, their differences made unmistakably sharp. The mother and father live vibrantly in their own right; at the same time, they unobtrusively symbolize the two central, conflicting forces in the novel: the human quest and its inevitable frustration.[4] Wolfe draws W. O. Gant in wonderful broad strokes: the long frame, the large hands, the great blade of a nose, the cold, uneasy eyes, the faint, sly grin at the corners of the thin mouth. Gant, a Northerner in the South, married to a woman he does not understand, longing to carve an angel's head, but unable to, desiring to be a Far Wanderer but tied to his family and home. Gant is "a stranger in a strange land." Sporadically drunk and disorderly, he is nevertheless the artist striving to impose order on a changing world. Gant brings a kind of ritual to their wild family life. Combining Shakespearean rhetoric with Southern political oratory, he delivers to wife and children carefully rehearsed speeches, full of invective, at appointed hours of the day. He yells:

[4] For a full discussion of this theme, see Louis D. Rubin, Jr., *Thomas Wolfe, The Weather of His Youth* (Baton Rouge: Louisiana State University Press, 1955).

We will freeze in this hellish, damnable, cruel and God-forsaken climate. Does Brother Will Care? Does Brother Jim care? Did the Old
Hog, your miserable old father, care? Merciful God! I have fallen into
the hands of fiends incarnate, more savage, more cruel, more abominable than the beasts of the field. Hellhounds that they are, they will
sit by and gloat at my agony until I am done to death.

Although the hand of death is ever upon him, he remains a fount
of energy: he is the great provider, buying whole hogs from the
butcher, and a marvelous gardener: "The earth was spermy for
him like a big woman." Gant builds roaring fires; his neighbors
can tell he is at home by the thick column of smoke from the chim-
ney. He is the source of sexual energy: twice-married father of eight,
old rooster frequenting Elizabeth's brothel, pursuer of colored cooks
and middle-aged widows, he is held in high esteem even by the
Temperance Ladies of the First Baptist Church. To his children he
is simply man as hero:

> swinging violently back and forth in a stout rocker, [he spits] clean
> and powerful spurts of tobacco-juice over his son's head into the hissing
> fire.

Eliza is her husband's antithesis. He disdains ownership, spends
lavishly, and talks rapidly. She, on the other hand, saves bits of
string; has a "powerful germinal instinct for property . . . [; and
likes] "to take her time" [and come] "to the point after interminable divagations down all the lane-ends of memory and overtone,
feasting upon the golden pageant of all she had ever said, done,
felt, thought, seen or replied, with egocentric delight." Her memory moves over the ocean bed of events like a great octopus. To
Gant, and at times to all the rest of the family, she seems to symbolize the immutable Time and inert matter that will inevitably
frustrate man's romantic quest. Yet she, too, is emphatically human
as she stands perpetually over the spitting grease, her nose "stove-
red," her hands chapped with hard work and covered with glycer-
ine, her body "clothed in a tattered old sweater and indefinable
under-lappings."

Wolfe particularly establishes her humanity in his account of
the death of Ben, surely the best prose that he ever wrote. Here

is language so accurate that it makes the reader see poor Ben in his last moments, language full of feeling yet seldom sentimental:

> the sallow yellow tint of his face had turned grey: out of this granite tint of death, lit by two red flags of fever, the stiff black furze of a three-day beard was growing . . . it recalled the corrupt vitality of hair, which can grow from a rotting corpse.

Wolfe brings the whole family together for the death: Helen contradicting herself, vibrating between rage at Eliza's ineptitude in the emergency and pity because Ben has rejected his mother; senile Gant, weeping in his rocker at the foot of Ben's bed, and employing his old rhetoric not to eulogize his son but to pity himself:

> O Jesus! I can't bear it! . . . How are we ever going to face this fearful and croo-el winter? It'll cost a thousand dollars before we're through burying him. . . .

Helen actually shaking him in fury right in the death chamber.

> And Eliza, now that [Ben] could deny her no longer . . . sitting near his head beside him, clutching his cold hand between her rough worn palms.

Even when Ben is apparently rigid in death, he asserts his vitality:

> suddenly, marvelously, as if his resurrection and rebirth had come upon him, Ben drew upon the air in a long and powerful respiration; his grey eyes opened. Filled with a terrible vision of all life in the one moment, he seemed to rise forward bodilessly from his pillows without support—a flame, a light, a glory—joined at length in death to the dark spirit who had brooded upon each footstep of his lonely adventure on earth.

But this is not all. Daringly, Wolfe follows the tragic account of Ben's death with a chapter full of eating and of comedy which ends in the funeral parlor of "Horse" Hines, beside Ben's embalmed corpse. Overcome with pride, Hines explains his artistry, how he has tried to do Ben justice. When Luke finds Ben a trifle pale, Hines whips out a rouge-stick and sketches a "ghastly rose-hued mockery of life and health" upon the dead grey cheeks. "Did you ever see anything more natural in your life?" Eugene notes "with a sort of tenderness . . . the earnestness and pride in the long horse-face." But the "dogs of laughter" tug at Eugene's throat, he slides gently off his chair, slowly unbuttoning his vest, languidly loosening his tie. He gurgles helplessly, and Luke looks on all a-grin. That Wolfe should introduce a comic note here is perfectly appropriate. It has been said that the essence of comedy is "human life-feeling." Wolfe, for all his loneliness, self-pity, and despair, affirmed life. He managed to pack a very great deal of this "human life-feeling" into *Look Homeward, Angel.* For this reason and despite countless obvious faults, the novel endures, and Wolfe appears to have conquered his old enemy Time, after all.

# You Can't Go Home Again: Thomas Wolfe and "The Escapes of Time and Memory"

*by Morris Beja*

. . . I know there is nothing so commonplace, so dull, that is
not touched with nobility and dignity. And I intend to wreak
out my soul on paper and express it all. This is what my life
means to me: I am at the mercy of this thing and I will do it or
die. I never forget; I have never forgotten.

Thomas Wolfe, *Letters to His Mother*[1]

Thomas Wolfe never forgot, had never forgotten: that, it turned
out, was his trouble. His realization late in his career that "you
can't go home again" had for Wolfe complex moral, social, and
psychological implications—but for his readers its chief interest is
in the *artistic* import that Wolfe gave to it. For as a statement about
art it emphatically denies the most sweeping assumption in Wolfe's
own work: that you can create valuable art by returning to your
personal past—indeed, by permitting your art to be "at the mercy
of" that past.

Wolfe had made this assumption ever since he had turned away
from his early attempts at writing drama and had begun to write
autobiographical novels. From then on, his work showed an overwhelming emphasis on his own recollections, intensified by his possession of so powerful a memory that he seemed capable of total
recall. His famous discussion in *The Story of a Novel* of the three

"You Can't Go Home Again: Thomas Wolfe and 'The Escapes of Time and
Memory,'" by Morris Beja. From *Modern Fiction Studies*, vol. 11, no. 3 (Autumn
1965), pp. 297–314. *Modern Fiction Studies* © 1965, by Purdue Research Foundation, Lafayette, Indiana. Reprinted by permission of the author and publisher.

[1] (New York, 1943), pp. 51–52.

elements of time—"actual present time," "past time," and "time immutable" [2]—has, I think, received more notice than it deserves. Systematic reasoning was not one of Wolfe's strengths, and his comments on time are after all neither profound in themselves nor very enlightening in terms of his own work. The one time element that really monopolized his attention was the past, together with one's memories of its individual moments. Although his preoccupation with it was closely related to many of his other important themes— notably the origins and functions of art, the search for a father, and the relationships between the South and the North, Europe and America—it towered above them all in significance.

In his records of the moments of his past, Wolfe was to a degree attempting what James Joyce's Stephen Dedalus meant by his conviction that the task of the artist is "to record . . . epiphanies with extreme care, seeing that they themselves are the most delicate and evanescent of moments." [3] Wolfe, of course, greatly admired Joyce's work; my point here is that he did so largely because he felt that Joyce was able to do successfully what he himself longed to do: he believed, for example, that in *Ulysses* "the effort to apprehend and to make live again a moment in lost time is so tremendous that . . . Joyce really did succeed, at least in places, in penetrating reality. . . ." [4] In *Of Time and the River,* Wolfe refers to this compulsion as "the intolerable desire to fix eternally in the patterns of an indestructible form a single moment of man's living, a single moment of life's beauty, passion, and unutterable eloquence, that passes, flames and goes." [5] In this essay, I shall try to examine the effect this attempt to fix forever moments of the past had on Wolfe's novels, and how it led him to—and illuminates—his eventual realization that, after all, you can't go home again. I pay particular attention to two of the most striking and pervasive forms his effort took: the "recapture" of the past; and the sudden attribution of new and immense significance to moments out of lost time which

---

[2] (New York, 1936), pp. 51–52.

[3] *Stephen Hero,* ed. Theodore Spencer, rev. John J. Slocum and Herbert Cahoon (Norfolk, Conn., 1963), p. 211. Cf. p. 32: "He sought in his verses to fix the most elusive of his moods. . . ."

[4] *Letters,* ed. Elizabeth Nowell (New York, 1956), p. 322.

[5] (New York, 1935), p. 551.

originally made no distinct impression whatsoever, and which may have seemed, indeed, all but forgotten.

In Marcel Proust's strict sense of the term, "recapturing" the past involves not merely recalling an event but actually living through it again in all its original reality, with all its physical and mental associations. During his privileged moments, consequently, it seems to Proust's Marcel that the past he relives fuses with the present and becomes contemporary with it, while Wolfe writes that once, when George Webber noticed the first signs of Spring, the color green so worked upon his memory that "the past became as real as the present, and he lived in the events of twenty years ago with as much intensity and as great a sense of actuality as if they had just occurred. He felt that there was no temporal past or present, no *now* more living than any reality of *then*. . . ." [6] Eugene Gant has the same experiences, and they always occur in an epiphany, suddenly: "always when that lost world would come back, it came at once, like a sword thrust through the entrails, in all its panoply of past time, living, whole, and magic as it had always been" (*Of Time and River*, p. 200). Not everyone, however, is capable of recapturing the past; it would seem that one must have a virtually abnormal awareness of the sensations of the present in order to feel them again when they have gone, or at least when most people would say they have "gone." One needs the almost neurotic ultra-sensibility of a Marcel—a quality already part of Eugene's make-up when he is "not quite six": "his sensory equipment was so complete that at the moment of perception of a single thing, the whole background of color, warmth, odor, sound, taste established itself, so that later, the breath of hot dandelion brought back the grass-warm banks of Spring, a day, a place, the rustling of young leaves, or the page of a book, the thin exotic smell of tangerine, the wintry bite of great apples. . . ." [7]

Wolfe believed that he himself possessed such a sensibility and that his memory was characterized "in a more than ordinary degree by the intensity of its sense impressions." As an illustration, he describes in *The Story of a Novel* how one day he was sitting in a Paris café, when suddenly and for no apparent reason he remem-

[6] *The Web and the Rock* (New York, 1958), p. 541.
[7] *Look Homeward, Angel* (New York, 1952), p. 84.

bered the iron railing on the boardwalk at Atlantic City: "I could
see it instantly just the way it was . . . It was all so vivid and
concrete that I could feel my hand upon it and know the exact dimensions, its size and weight and shape" (pp. 31–32). Wolfe asserts
that this experience—and others like it, all of which also took place,
paradoxically, in Europe—enabled him to discover his America,
which he had begun to feel was lost to him. Both his fictional
counterparts also undergo the same discovery while in France: the
incident that causes Eugene to look homeward occurs toward the
end of *Of Time and the River,* when a church-bell in Dijon brings
him back to the bell in college at Pulpit Hill, and then even further
back to his childhood and "the lost America" (p. 898); the incident
that takes George home again occurs in Boulogne, as he enters a
hotel room for the first time yet "feels that he has been here before"—in a sensation of *déjà vu* very similar to what happens at the
beginning of Proust's privileged moments—and then revives an
evening in the Old Catawba of twenty years before (*Web and Rock,*
pp. 631–632).

In the other kind of moment rescued from lost time stressed by
Wolfe, an event produces a revelation, but only long after the event
itself has occurred—in what might be called a moment of delayed
revelation, or a "restrospective" epiphany. Such moments are so
numerous in the novels of Thomas Wolfe that it would be pointless
to quote many examples here; they form the bulk of the long catalogues of Eugene's and George's memories that fill so many pages
in his books. And *The Story of a Novel* describes how, when Wolfe
began to work on the first book of an intended series, he compiled
vast lists of almost every conceivable sort, as if he strove in some
way to find in the material details and fleeting trivia of the past the
sense of value and permanence for which he longed. Some of these
lists were put among sections of his manuscripts headed by the
words "Where now?":

> Under such a heading as this, there would be brief notations of those
> thousands of things which all of us have seen for just a flash, a moment
> in our lives, which seem to be of no consequence whatever at the mo-
> ment that we see them, and which live in our minds and hearts forever,
> which are somehow pregnant with all the joy and sorrow of the human
> destiny, and which we know, somehow, are therefore more important

than many things of more apparent consequence. "Where now?"
(pp. 43–44)

Where now?: the question figures not only in Wolfe's manuscripts,
but in the catalogues recorded in the published versions of his novels as well.[8] Like his desire and evident ability to recapture lost
time, it reflects the general infatuation with the past that Wolfe
brought to his art when he first began to write novels.

Art reflects the mind and world of its creator in more ways than
one; while many of the moments of intense emotion in *Look Homeward, Angel* are based, as everyone is aware, on the actual remembrance of things past by its young author, a large number of its apparently purely imaginary incidents also involve the recollection or
recapture of lost time, by various characters themselves. Oliver Gant
goes through such a moment when, to his dismay, the local madam
buys his statue of an angel for a prostitute's grave. The importance
to Gant of this angel has been prepared for by the first epiphany in
the novel—one which, significantly, dealt with the discovery of artistic longings. Gant, fifteen years old, was walking along a street
in Philadelphia when he saw a statue of an angel outside a stone
cutter's shop, and it instilled a lifelong desire "to wreak something
dark and unspeakable in him into cold stone," to "carve an angel's
head," to "seek the great forgotten language, the lost lane-end into
heaven" (p. 3). The angel purchased by the madam is not the same
one; it has been imported from Italy. But it is as close as Gant has
ever come to carving his own angel and to finding the forgotten
language. As he and the madam conclude their transaction, their
thoughts turn to the years that have gone by since their youth. They
look out upon the town square, where everything seems suddenly
"frozen in a picture": "And in that second the slow pulse of the
fountain was suspended, life was held, like an arrested gesture, in
photographic abeyance, and Gant felt himself alone move death-
ward in a world of seemings as, in 1910, a man might find himself
again in a picture taken on the grounds of the Chicago Fair, when
he was thirty and his mustache black, and, noting the bustled ladies
and the derbied men fixed in the second's pullulation, remember

---

[8] See, e.g., *Look Homeward, Angel*, pp. 203, 285; *The Web and the Rock*, p. 276.

the dead instant, seek beyond the borders for what was there. . . ." "Where now?" Wolfe asks, "Where after? Where then?" (p. 285).

At the end of the novel, Gant's son Eugene sees in the same square a vision of his entire past and all his younger selves, in a scene apparently meant to illustrate Wolfe's assertion in his note to the reader that "we are the sum of all the moments of our lives" (p. xvii):

> And for a moment all the silver space was printed with the thousand forms of himself and Ben. There, by the corner in from Academy Street, Eugene watched his own approach; there, by the City Hall, he strode with lifted knees; there, by the curb upon the step, he stood, peopling the night with the great lost legion of himself—the thousand forms that came, that passed, that wove and shifted in unending change, and that remained unchanging Him.

> And through the Square, unwoven from lost time, the fierce bright horde of Ben spun in and out its deathless loom. Ben, in a thousand moments, walked the Square: Ben of the lost years, the forgotten days, the unremembered hours. . . . And now the Square was thronging with their lost bright shapes, and all the minutes of lost time collected and stood still. Then, shot from them with projectile speed, the Square shrank down the rails of destiny, and was vanished with all things done, with all forgotten shapes of himself and Ben. (pp. 658–659)

When the images of the past have disappeared, Eugene experiences another "moment of terrible vision," this time of "his foiled quest of himself," of the same hunger that has "darkened his father's eyes to impalpable desire for wrought stone and the head of an angel"; we are thus brought back to the first epiphany in the novel. Ben reveals in an "apexical summation" that what Eugene seeks must be found within himself ("*You* are your world"), and that the object of his quest—"the forgotten language, the lost world" (pp. 660–662)—involves the past as much as the future. But it is forward that Eugene tries to look as he expresses in his final words his confidence that he will some day find what he desires, just as at the end of *The Story of a Novel* Wolfe himself is confident that we may all "find the tongue, the language, and the conscience that as men and artists we have got to have" (p. 93). The last chapter of the novel has generally suggested the visions in Joyce's Nighttown episode in *Ulysses*; but it is Stephen Dedalus' affirmation on the last page of *A Portrait of the Artist*—that, as artificer, he will forge the uncreated conscience of his race—that is called to mind by the last page of *Look Homeward, Angel,* with the young artist's determination to attain what his father has sought but never found in the carved angel: "the forgotten language, the lost world."

In general significance and radiance, this final vision and the others I have cited are exceptions to most of the frozen moments of new enlightenment in the book, which are plentiful and often individually effective, but which too frequently have no real function in relation to the rest of the novel. They reveal a good deal about specific people, but little in regard to comprehensive themes, and they sometimes even seem like merely irrelevant intrusions, included for no other reason than that they personally interest the novelist; the result is that they contribute toward one's impression of the novel as a compilation of fragments. Occasionally, however, as at the end, a moment of revelation will not only give us insight into one of Wolfe's characters, but also serve broader purposes of form by bringing together various themes or threads in the story.

Such structural weaknesses in the use of epiphanies are in one way alleviated in *Of Time and the River,* where a measure of unity is provided by the fact that many of Eugene's visions occur while he is a passenger on a train, as he looks out a window onto an evanescent world which disappears as soon as he has seen it, but the sight of which has a permanent effect upon him; often, for example, glimpses of people whom he will never see again powerfully impress upon Eugene, as his train rushes past them, a sense of the essential isolation in which we all live. Railroad journeys occur throughout the novel, and such visions connect all its sections, early, middle, or late, whether the action takes place in the South or in the North, in America or in Europe. They also help integrate *Of Time and the River* as a whole into the sequence of volumes that tell the life story of the Wolfe hero, for no symbol is more pervasive in Wolfe's work than the train. But in none of the other novels do they play so large a role in providing a degree of internal coherence; in fact, a more appropriate title for the book might well have been *Of Time and the Railroad,* for the image of the river does not even approach in importance that of the train. Wolfe himself, when he tries to describe the "design" of the novel, does not refer to the continuous flow of a river, but is forced instead into the realization that he "can liken these chapters only to a row of lights which one sometimes sees at night from the windows of a speeding train" (*Story of Novel*, p. 54). As this remark suggests, the limited coherence achieved by the image of the railroad and the visions centering on it is more than offset by the disjointed effect created when countless revelations of all types run through the novel with little or no attempt at relating most of them to each other.

Wolfe's problems in this regard are further compounded by the novel's climax. *Look Homeward, Angel* had at least ended with a powerful and unifying vision; *Of Time and the River* ends with what is probably the chief example in Wolfe of a non-functional and even harmful epiphany, one which seems completely out of place in the novel it is meant to conclude. In the final scene, Eugene is leaving Europe and returning to America; he is in a small boat with a number of other people, waiting to board the ship that is to take them home. All the travelers feel the strange power of the huge liner as it towers over them, but Wolfe gives special attention to the effect of this "magic moment" on a woman named Esther, whom we have never encountered before. We are then shown her own effect on Eugene, as he turns toward her; from the moment he sees her, his spirit is "impaled upon the knife of love." As if that were not bad enough, "at that instant" he also loses the "wild integrity" and the "proud inviolability of youth" (pp. 910–911). Whereupon the novel ends. As the conclusion to an already ill-structured book, this revelation, which should form the forceful climax to the entire novel, succeeds only in leaving the reader hanging in the air. Eugene's loss of his youth can hardly be regarded as a dramatic or convincing corollary of what amounts to an epiphany of love at first sight. Besides, Wolfe's hero instantaneously loses his youth forever very often, and in this case the supposed loss is so unpersuasive as to be embarrassing. One would like to be able to find some alternative thematic function served by this incident: to regard it, say, as a culmination of the search for a mother—which, despite Wolfe's claim that the controlling idea in *Of Time and the River* is "man's search to find a father" (*Story of Novel*, p. 39), often seems as central in his work as the father theme. But the scene does not really fit this interpretation either, and though eventually Esther does in some degree become a mother figure, that role is of course not evident until the George Webber novels. Indeed, no matter how one looks at it, this scene is so unrelated to the context of the rest of the novel that it can only be regarded as a passage that starts threads that are entirely new. Strictly speaking, moreover, those threads were never taken up and no sequel to the book was ever written, for Wolfe never published another novel about Eugene Gant—though in the end, to be sure, we must ignore Wolfe's switch from Eugene to George Webber.

One of the most frequently cited causes of the structural defects of *Of Time and the River,* and of Wolfe's other novels as well, has been his inability or unwillingness to control the flow of memories he so freely permitted himself to record in his fiction—so freely that the flow became a deluge. Of course, Wolfe was correct in believing that there is much to be said for what he called, in a famous letter to F. Scott Fitzgerald, the "putter-inner" (as opposed to the "leaver-outer") approach to fiction (*Letters,* p. 643). But this approach also entails great dangers, and too often Wolfe's own work does not overcome his obsession to be a putter-inner of everything. Yet it is an oversimplification to say that Wolfe's "chief fault," in his own words, was merely that he "wrote too much" (*Story of Novel,* p. 83); a lack of critical judgment was also involved. He devoted so much space to autobiographical details which the reader can only regard as at best unessential that his novels frequently give the impression—valid or not—that he failed to understand that not every moment personally important to him need also be artistically significant. To Wolfe, all the myriad experiences he gives his hero are important, even essential; all of them at least potentially involve revelations. And the ones explicitly described as revelations are so numerous as to appear in almost every scene. By itself, each might be fully credible—but not as simply one out of a massive crowd; under such conditions, they take on something of the character of a mere artistic "convention." And Wolfe aggravates his difficulties by treating every one of the illuminations as if it were of cosmic proportions. Instead of subordinating some of them in comparison with others, he uses the same superlative adjectives to describe what would seem to be relatively unimportant moments of insight as he uses in the accounts of those he obviously regards as vital or climactic, such as the ones which end all his novels. We are so frequently told that this or that moment will never be forgotten and produces a revelation completely changing the course of Eugene's life that each such passage loses much of its intended force, and after a while we begin to treat these statements with skepticism—perhaps we even cease to notice some of them.

After the publication of *Of Time and the River,* Wolfe became increasingly conscious of the dangers inherent in his striving for all-inclusiveness. *The Story of a Novel,* having described the manuscripts included under the heading of "Where now?," suddenly rejects both them and the uncontrolled use of memory they seem to imply. In an unexpected and disconcertingly brief passage, Wolfe writes:

> It may be objected, it has been objected already by certain critics, that in such research as I have here attempted to describe there is a quality of intemperate excess, an almost insane hunger to devour the entire body of human experience, to attempt to include more, experience more, than the measure of one life can hold, or than the limits of a single work of art can well define. I readily admit the validity of this criticism. I think I realize as well as any one the fatal dangers that are consequent to such a ravenous desire, the damage it may wreak upon one's life and on one's work. . . .
>
> . . . And now I really believe that so far as the artist is concerned, the unlimited extent of human experience is not so important for him as the depth and intensity with which he experiences things. (pp. 46–47)

As here presented, Wolfe's new attitude is as yet vague and undefined, but it does suggest a stronger realization that his work has suffered from his lack of selectivity. It is of course inconceivable that Thomas Wolfe could ever really have become a leaver-outer. But though the "Where now?" method was inevitable and even justifiable for the early stages of his particular career, he now sees that it must be modified so as to take into consideration the quality of remembered experience as much as, or even more than, its quantity; not every event that had occurred to him is worthy of being recorded in art as what I have called a retrospective epiphany.

This new point of view indicates a degree of reaction against the almost completely free play he had thus far given his memory in the fictional chronicle of his life; and therefore, as far as it goes, it is a sign of Wolfe's transition from the attitude we have seen in his youthful letter to his mother—"I intend to wreak out my soul on paper and express it all. . . . I never forget; I have never forgotten"—to his eventual conviction that you can't go home again. I say "as far as it goes" because in itself this passage is anything but a clear and emphatic statement, and its context contains further qualifications. Nevertheless, it is one of the first signs of a significant shift in his thinking.

There are a few less questionable signs in his next published volume, though again only a few. *The Web and the Rock,* like *You Can't Go Home Again* (Wolfe, of course, meant them to form a single novel), was never corrected or even finished by Wolfe himself, and it had to be posthumously edited by Edward C. Aswell. Much of it, moreover, was written as early as *Of Time and the River,* and it is therefore doubly difficult to depend on it in order to trace the development of Wolfe's techniques and ideas. However, we do know that except for a few passages, notably the ending, the last half was written before the first, though he did rewrite "small portions of it" before he died.[9] This situation leads to some awkward discrepancies between various viewpoints expressed within the novel itself, as well as with what Wolfe had said elsewhere. Conflicts are especially apparent in his comments on the role of memory in George Webber's art, and readers who have read *The Story of a Novel* carefully, but who are unaware of the peculiarities in the chronology of composition of *The Web and the Rock,* will be particularly struck by a number of passages in the novel that contradict the position toward which Wolfe had seemed to be groping. Thus, in the second (earlier) half of the book, Wolfe occasionally speaks approvingly of George's great reliance upon his powers of recollection, which make the past "as real as the present" (p. 541). "The majestic powers of memory," we are told, "exerted a benefi-

---

[9] Edward C. Aswell, "A Note on Thomas Wolfe," in Wolfe, *The Hills Beyond* (New York, 1941), p. 374. But for a full discussion of the composition of Wolfe's work, see Richard S. Kennedy, *The Window of Memory: The Literary Career of Thomas Wolfe* (Chapel Hill, N. C., 1962).

cent and joyful dominion over his life, sharpening and making intensely vivid every experience of each passing day," and enabling him to remember "a thousand fleeting and indefinable things which he had seen for the flick of an eye in some lost and dateless moment of the swarming past" (pp. 455–456). Yet such remarks, though published after Wolfe's death, are not indications of a late reversion to the attitude that had produced the "Where now?" catalogues, but are rather another early product of that attitude. The newly written sections of the book, in contrast, reflect Wolfe's more recent concern about the pernicious effect on his work of his emphasis on memory. When George begins to write his first novel, his memory is said to have grown so "encyclopaedic" and preoccupied with the "minutest details" that it impairs his art and becomes, "instead of a mighty weapon," a "gigantic, fibrous, million-rooted plant of time which spread and flowered like a cancerous growth." Eventually, as George begins to realize that he has been trying "to pour the ocean in a sanitary drinking cup," he does attempt to set down merely "a fractional part of his vision of the earth" (pp. 262–263). However, he is not really prepared to control the crushing power of his past, much less to discard it, and in another year his modest effort has—and Wolfe repeats his previous phrase—"spread and flowered like a cancerous growth": "From his childhood he could remember all that people said or did, but as he tried to set it down his memory opened up enormous vistas and associations, going from depth to limitless depth, until the simplest incident conjured up a buried continent of experience, and he was overwhelmed by a project of discovery and revelation that would have broken the strength and used up the lives of a regiment of men" (p. 273). We have here a description of essentially the same power as the one that had previously been depicted as exerting over George "a beneficent and joyful dominion," only now there is a marked difference in outlook toward its desirability. But though this and similar statements are significant, they are still isolated, infrequent, and counterbalanced by the passages that sharply contradict them.

A more pronounced symptom of Wolfe's doubts about his reliance on his own past in his fiction was his adoption of a new hero, whom he gave a childhood quite different from his own. This attempt to abandon strict autobiography was, perhaps inevitably, abortive; but it did bring him face to face with one of his most important failings—the almost complete absence from his work of objectivity. The novelist who works in the autobiographical form should not only be able to select the significant from the inconsequential; he should also be able to look at himself and his hero with a certain amount of perspective. And if he records his own epiphanies, as Joyce says it is for the man of letters to do, he will be most successful if he can do so with the impersonal self-analysis of a Proust, a Conrad, or of Joyce himself. Wolfe's treatment of many of his, on the other hand, is romanticized and theatrical. It would be absurd to condemn his novels because they are autobiographical. But it would, I am afraid, be correct to accuse them of being *too* autobiographical, in the sense that he seems to have seen his hero first as a reflection of himself, and then as a character in a work of art: he usually—though by no means always—failed to achieve that unique blend of subjective interest and objective insight that Edward Bullough called Psychical Distance.

Extreme subjectivity controls not only Wolfe's own attitude toward his experiences, but also the attitudes of his heroes toward theirs. Far from attaining any true and balanced view of the world around them during their moments of revelation, at such times they frequently have a view that is if anything even more individual and distorted than usual. They can see neither themselves nor others in perspective: they are self-deluded as well as self-absorbed. Their egotism is so excessive, and they are so unable to look at the world except through their own highly distorted glasses, that the credibility of their moments of supposed insight into the lives of other people is greatly affected, and despite the many moments in which Eugene or George feels an overpowering communion with other people, one's general impression is that of a bitter man more capable of abhorrence than of sympathy. For every stranger in the streets of Boston or New York to whom he feels his heart go out, there is someone, barely an acquaintance perhaps, whom he knows and—consequently—hates, fears, and despises. As a result, the sudden insights during which he is said to fathom completely some person or object are frequently unconvincing, for we find ourselves wondering if he is really capable of such insights. Generally, his

abnormally self-centered relationships with other people, and his
consequent inability to understand or communicate with them except on his own very peculiar terms and according to his own unusual needs, lessen the stature of the Wolfe hero as a human being;
specifically, they lessen the seriousness with which we can react to
some of his most important epiphanies, for we tend to regard his
moments of compassion as more rhetorical than real.

The rhetoric of the epiphanies at the end of *The Web and the
Rock,* when George confronts not someone else but his own reflection in a mirror, is an especially interesting example of some of
Wolfe's major tendencies, including his inclination to take his hero
too seriously, and his technical handling of moments of revelation.
George is in a hospital in Munich after having participated in a
brawl at the October Fair. His face has been beaten into an awful
sight, but as he looks at it in the mirror across from his bed he suddenly grins, and then laughs: "The battered mask laughed with
him, and at last his soul was free. He was a man" (p. 690). After
that last remark, we too are inclined to grin, and perhaps laugh.
As we have seen, this is not the first of the spiritual *bar mitzvahs*
Wolfe gives his heroes—nor is it the last, for that matter. But the
embarrassingly mawkish today-I-am-a-man quality of this scene is
particularly noticeable. Then, for the final epiphany, the reflection
even becomes vocal, and he and George have a dialogue—their talk,
as might be expected, centering on the past: George lovingly describes to his image his memories of childhood, the "good time."
"But," the reflection reveals in the very last words of the novel,
"you can't go home again" (p. 695). As a climactic epiphany, this
scene is almost as inadequate as the end of *Of Time and the River,*
and for essentially the same reasons. It is unprepared for and in its
context even seems irrelevant. The revelation it produces seems
artificially imposed and is not in the least convincing as the conclusion of all that has preceded it, much of which it in fact appears
to contradict. One is therefore not surprised to learn that this scene
was probably written much later than most of the last half of *The
Web and the Rock*[10]—which dates from the period of *Of Time and*

[10] Louis D. Rubin, Jr., says that Edward C. Aswell, the editor of Wolfe's post-
humous manuscripts, has written to Rubin of his agreement that this scene must
have been composed after the bulk of the last two novels (*Thomas Wolfe: The*

*the River,* before Wolfe himself had actually come to believe that you can't go home again. Of course, Wolfe did not intend that his manuscript be split in two here, so he can hardly be blamed for the inappropriateness of this scene to its final position, though as the novel stands it is nonetheless inappropriate. It is also ineffectual and unsatisfactory in itself, despite the fact that Wolfe regarded the whole episode of the October Fair as one of the most central in all his work. At one time, he even planned to use *The October Fair* as the title of the novel dealing with the period of his life covered by both *Of Time and the River* and *The Web and the Rock.*

It is not until the end of *You Can't Go Home Again* that, for the first time since *Look Homeward, Angel,* we have an effective climactic epiphany in one of Wolfe's novels. George, having returned to his beloved Germany as a famous author, is now on a train leaving it once more. At Aachen, the last stop before the border, he and the other travelers in his compartment are shocked to see that one of their fellow passengers—a nervous little man, whom George has privately called Fuss-and-Fidget—has been seized by the authorities. The rumor circulates that he is a Jew caught trying to escape with all his money. As the terrified little man tries to persuade the officers to let him go, since there must be some misunderstanding, he is led past his former traveling companions, his eyes glancing at them for just a moment. But he does not betray them by showing in any way that he knows them, and they board the train, leaving him behind on the platform.

> And the little man . . . paused once from his feverish effort to explain. As the car in which he had been riding slid by, he lifted his pasty face and terror-stricken eyes, and for a moment his lips were stilled of their anxious pleading. He looked once, directly and steadfastly, at his former companions, and they at him. And in that gaze there was all the unmeasured weight of man's mortal anguish. George and the others felt somehow naked and ashamed, and somehow guilty. They all felt that they were saying farewell, not to a man, but to humanity; not to some pathetic stranger, some chance acquaintance of the voyage, but

*Weather of His Youth,* Baton Rouge, 1955, pp. 176–177). On Aswell's editorial decisions in respect to the ending of *The Web and the Rock,* see Kennedy, *Window of Memory,* p. 390.

to mankind; not to some nameless cipher out of life, but to the fading image of a brother's face.

The train swept out and gathered speed—and so they lost him.[11]

As so often before, Wolfe has used a scene envisioned from a train window to dramatize a symbolic isolation. But this time the person seen is not a complete stranger; he has had some sort of contact with George and the other passengers. Perhaps that is why this isolated, helpless little man becomes in the end less an image of solitude than of the unity of all mankind. He has achieved a bond —even an identity—with all men, but especially with the people in the train. He is not even aware of it, and it would be little comfort to him if he were. But it is apparently of the greatest importance to those who see him; and, paradoxically, he could never have attained this bond were he not isolated and manifestly doomed.

This episode is one of the best things Wolfe ever did. Its power does not so much rely on the impassioned rhetoric so frequent in his work—though there is still some rhetoric, of the quieter sort— as on its relative calm, the frighteningly low key of its presentation. Even the discussion of the personal significance of the incident for George is treated concisely and with restraint. And the long letter to Foxhall Edwards that then closes the novel discussing some of the broader ramifications of this experience is also handled relatively well; though it follows the climax, it does not really seem anti-climactic. For we soon understand that this event does more than simply reveal to George the true nature of Nazi Germany or even teach him about humanity, though it does both these things; it goes much further and teaches him about himself, enables him to see himself with an objectivity he has never previously known. It thus prepares him for the evaluation of his entire life and career that he undertakes in the letter to Fox. And when we begin to see the full significance of all he has learned, we realize that if this vision of a brother may be compared in effectiveness to Eugene's vision of Ben at the end of *Look Homeward, Angel,* it must be contrasted to it in theme. For instead of involving the recapture of the past, it centers on the future: "He saw now that you can't go home again—not ever. There was no road back. . . . And there

[11] (New York, 1949), p. 699.

came to him a vision of man's true home, beyond the ominous and cloud-engulfed horizon of the here and now, in the green and hopeful and still-virgin meadows of the future" (p. 704). The little man's capture has been for George a catalytic agent producing a violent reaction against much that he has taken for granted in the past—and, even more important, against his great emphasis upon that past itself. You can't go home again. This time the phrase is packed with implications.

George's new discovery comes to him as a sudden shock despite the fact that he has already supposedly learned in a moment of revelation that "you can't go home again"; for the passage at the end of *The Web and the Rock* is a careless addition, as well as a late one. It is completely inconsistent with subsequent passages in *You Can't Go Home Again,* throughout which it is clear that George has yet to discover the truth of this phrase, though he occasionally comes close. Early in the novel, on a train heading toward Libya Hill, he meets Judge Rumford Bland, a figure of evil but also of a kind of dark wisdom. "And do you think," Bland asks him, "you can go home again?" (p. 83). George's hesitant, "almost frightened" affirmative response ("Why—why yes! Why—") makes it clear that he has not yet had the new awareness attributed to him at the end of the *The Web and the Rock,* that he still has much to learn, but that he is already beginning to be uncomfortable. He realizes that Bland's question refers not merely to the physical act of returning to the town of Libya Hill, and he is beginning to suspect—and this thought represents no less than a revolution in Wolfe's ideas—that lost time cannot be recaptured. Indeed, this discovery is the one that George finally makes at the end of the novel, when it is stated not simply as an inevitable fact, but also as a moral principle: you *ought* not to recapture the past, you *must* not go home again. The attempt to do so is not merely futile; it is wrong. I do not mean to imply that Wolfe rejects the past itself; that would be absurd and useless. Nor does he repudiate his "home" when he sadly realizes that he cannot go there again. Rather, he rejects the idea that you can or should re-live the past, that it can entirely control your life and art.

Wolfe had once written to Julian Meade of his emphatic conviction that "in no sense of the word" could writing be considered "an escape from reality"; in fact, it is "an attempt to approach and penetrate reality." As an example of what he meant, he cited *Ulysses,* with its "effort to apprehend and to make live again a moment in lost time" (*Letters,* pp. 321–322). But Joyce had been able to exercise strict control over this effort, while Wolfe, as he himself now saw, had made it almost his sole preoccupation. Consequently, he had so distorted its importance that it had become "an escape from reality" after all. The means of escape were the things that make up the mysterious dream world of what used to be. Wolfe described the essence of his new knowledge in a letter written a few months before his fatal illness to Edward C. Aswell, who adapted Wolfe's words for the bridge between the German episode of the little man and George's letter to Fox:

> . . . the whole book might almost be called "You Can't Go Home Again"—which means back home to one's family, back home to one's childhood, back home to the father one has lost, back home to romantic love, to a young man's dreams of glory and of fame, back home to exile, to escape to "Europe" and some foreign land, back home to lyricism, singing just for singing's sake, back home to aestheticism, to one's youthful ideas of the "artist," and the all-sufficiency of "art and beauty and love," back home to the ivory tower, back home to places in the country, the cottage in Bermuda away from all the strife and conflict of the world, back home to the father one is looking for —to someone who can help one, save one, ease the burden for one, back home to the old forms and systems of things that once seemed everlasting, but that are changing all the time—back home to the escapes of Time and Memory. . . . But the conclusion is not sad: this is a hopeful book—the conclusion is that although you can't go home again, the home of every one of us is in the future: there is no other way.[12]

The "escapes of Time and Memory" comprehend all the others, and the radical nature of his departure from them, with all its personal, moral, and artistic implications, was not lost upon Wolfe—nor upon George, who admits to Edwards: "No man that I have known was ever more deeply rooted in the soil of Time and Memory . . . than was I" (*You Can't Go Home Again,* p. 739).

To Wolfe, the notion that you can't go home again applies spe-

---

[12] Pp. 711–712. Cf. *You Can't Go Home Again,* p. 706.

cifically to *art* in two principal ways: in its essentially moral statement that you can't use art itself as an escape from reality; and,
more important for its complete reversal of Wolfe's former views,
in its essentially aesthetic statement that you can't create worthwhile art through the particular escapes of Time and Memory.
Wolfe had already come to the realization that a novelist must be
selective in his use of the past; perhaps because he has as yet been
unable to put this realization into practice to his own satisfaction,
he now suspects that one must not use the past at all, and his statements suggest a belief that the attempt to base one's art upon personal memories is *always* mistaken, even if carried out with the
utmost selection and control: "He saw now that you can't go home
again—not ever" (p. 704). He thus reacts against his former methods even more forcefully than reason might have dictated, though
in his case such a fierce reaction is perhaps necessary. In the letter
to Fox, George laughs at all the people who have spread rumors
that he would never be able to start another novel. The ironic
truth is that he has found it impossible to finish anything; his trouble, far from being an inability to begin, is an inability to stop recording all he remembers. His "huge inheritance" had become a
"giant web" in which he had entrapped himself; in admitting this
to Fox, George repeats the phrases that had become so familiar in
Wolfe's novels: "forgotten memories exhumed . . . until I lived
them in my dreams," "nothing that had ever been was lost," "I lived
again through all times and weathers I had known," "the forgotten
moments and unnumbered hours came back" (p. 740). But though
this langauge has appeared before, and despite George's obvious
relish in reverting to it, there is now an unshrinking recognition
that his "torrential recollectiveness" has been a burden, has brought
about a distorted attitude toward life and art, and has produced
a "million-fibered integument" which has bound him to the past
and therefore stifled his creativity.

Wolfe's statements are not specific enough for us to be able to
tell the extent to which he consciously intended his new position
as a criticism of all that he himself had so far written, but it is natural that his readers look at it in terms of the light it sheds upon
Wolfe's accomplishments. One's attitude toward it necessarily involves an evaluation of Wolfe's entire career; in so far as one re-

gards the view taken at the end of *You Can't Go Home Again* as valid, then so much lower must his estimate be of all of Wolfe's novels, for that view rejects their very basis: the assumption that you can return to the past. But it is not a perfectly simple matter to judge the validity of Wolfe's notion that he had been wrong to try to go home again, for though his memory produced some of the most glaring of his artistic defects, it often contributed much of the value and uniqueness his novels do have. It was at times his strength and at times his weakness. . . .

Actually, it is doubtful whether Wolfe ever would or could have given up autobiographical fiction; and it is at least questionable whether his future work would have been better if he had. One suspects he would have discovered that, like Orpheus, he had to look back whatever the cost. And if in the end Wolfe had found himself unable to write effectively about anything but the memorable moments out of his own past, regardless of all the dangers they entailed, he surely would have gone back to them with little hesitation—he was never one to be entrapped by a consistency, especially a foolish one. But his growing awareness of the dangers inherent in his use of such moments might have led him at last beyond a mere lip-service recognition of the need to control Time and Memory rather than to continue to let his art be controlled by them. He might have come to treat them as tools, not escapes— to create the great novel he never wrote, but which he had it in him to write.

# Thomas Wolfe and the American Experience

## by Richard S. Kennedy

Over the years I have spent so much time acquainting myself
with the life and writings of Thomas Wolfe that I have grown rather
weary of him. He has been to me like a house-guest who arrived one
day fifteen years ago and then proceeded to make himself a member
of the family. If he were a jolly, healthy-minded, companionable
fellow, it would perhaps be all right, but artists seldom are. In spite
of his gusto, he is self-centered, neurotic, and garrulous. I grew sick
of his presence. I thought I would get him to move out when I finally
published my book about him. But lo! I found myself inviting him
to stay on. Apparently I have learned to live with him as I have
learned to live with myself. Now, with the help of my friend Paschal
Reeves of the University of Georgia, I am engaged in editing Wolfe's
pocket notebooks.

The William B. Wisdom Collection of Thomas Wolfe materials,
housed in the Harvard Library, has thirty-five of Wolfe's pocket
notebooks plus a few fragments of a couple of others.[1] They vary in
size. They are all somewhat smudged and dog-eared. Wolfe carried
them around in his pockets intermittently from 1926 when he was
beginning his first novel, *Look Homeward, Angel,* until just before
his death when he took a trip by automobile through a dozen national parks in the Great American West.

These notebooks constitute the most fascinating body of material

"Thomas Wolfe and the American Experience," by Richard S. Kennedy. From
*Modern Fiction Studies*, vol. 11, no. 3 (Autumn 1965), pp. 219–33. *Modern Fiction
Studies* © 1965, by Purdue Research Foundation, Lafayette, Indiana. Reprinted
by permission of the author and publisher.

[1] There are also pages of notations in other forms, on loose sheets or in large
accounting ledgers, which will be used in the edition of Wolfe's notebooks. The
framework of the edition, however, will be the pocket notebooks.

in the entire Wisdom Collection. They are not diaries—like Pepy's or Evelyn's. They are not journals—like those that Thoreau or Gide or Hawthorne kept. They are not like the working commonplace books that Henry James or Somerset Maugham kept. They are not even exactly like Coleridge's (though parts of them resemble Coleridge's very much). They are to my mind unique. They are a combination of the evidences of daily living, the informal records of a literary career, and jottings which afford glimpses into the psyche of Thomas Wolfe. To be specific, the notebooks are a jumble (in the way that life is a jumble and that the unconscious and preconscious realm of the human psyche is a jumble) of literary ideas, outlines of literary projects, character sketches, first drafts of passages which later turn up in the novels, observations jotted down while traveling, diary passages, first drafts of letters (some of which he never sent), opinions about social questions (politics, religion, race, etc.), meditations and generalizations about his own life and about human behavior, opinions about contemporary literary figures, notes on books that he read, records of dreams, records of conversations overheard in restaurants or bars, notes on telephone conversations, lists (of mountains seen, rivers crossed, states and countries visited, women who were important to him, books read, restaurants dined in, people met), jottings in which he is using his notebook as a way of talking to himself or arguing with himself, lists of books to buy, grocery lists, laundry lists, telephone numbers, American Express numbers, assignments for his N.Y.U. students, and so on. In other words, the notebooks reflect the experience both trivial and valuable of a writer's life. Further, they show Wolfe in a variety of moods from the heights of exuberance to the glooms of despair, from intense and irrational anger to rollicking good humor.

The richness of this source of information about Wolfe's life, about his work, and about his associations in the literary scene of the twenties and thirties is such that one hopes it will stimulate a whole new series of Wolfe studies. I myself have been tempted to follow out a number of threads of interest which have their beginning in the notebooks. The one which has fascinated me most prompts me to offer here some observations on Thomas Wolfe and the experience of being an American writer.

I will begin by reminding readers of some distinctive features of

Wolfe as a literary figure. His work is largely autobiographical fiction, accounts done in a highly elevated style of the adventures of a superhuman character named Eugene Gant or George Webber. It has always been difficult for critics to call these works novels, for each one is, to some extent, an encyclopedic assembly of literary phenomena—encyclopedic in the sense that Melville's *Moby Dick* is an encyclopedic prose work and Whitman's *Song of Myself* is an encyclopedic work in verse. Also Thomas Wolfe's writings have been regarded as having an "American" quality in the same way that we think of the work of Jean-Paul Sartre as distinctly French, or of John Galsworthy as distinctly British, or of J. M. Synge as distinctly Irish.

It seems to me that Wolfe's notebooks provide a new perspective on some of these features of Wolfe's work. The notebooks show us in great detail how an American artist who was as naively self-conscious of his national identity as if he were a contemporary of George Bancroft or Daniel Webster equipped himself to be a writer and strove to cope with what he conceived to be the problems of an American writer.

The national consciousness is continually expressed in his notebooks. Frequent entries appear during his European travels. Sometimes it is as abrupt and enigmatic as his jotting: "My name is Wolfe. I am an American." [2] Other times he will draw comparisons between Europeans and Americans, as for example when he notes: "*The French*—they are literally unconscious of the rest of the world. They know nothing of its extent, of the 16,000 miles of sea, of its grandeur, its diversity, its immensity. They are completely contained within themselves—their certitude comes from the rigid and narrow limit of their life, which does not seem rigid and narrow to them. . . . For this reason, Americans who play the monkey to them are fools. For even the dullest American has the sea in his mind, and the immensity of his own country." [3] He felt that there was something effete about Europe, that it no longer had any cultural directions.

[2] Pocket Notebook 31, Aug. 20, 1936, to *ca.* Sept. 30, 1936. In further notes, the term Pocket Notebook will be abbreviated to PN.

All quotations from Wolfe's unpublished writings which appear in the present article are made with the permission of the administrator of the Estate of Thomas Wolfe. Mr. Paul Gitlin, 5 West 45th Street, New York, N. Y. Further quotation of these excerpts will require a similar special grant of permission.

[3] PN 3, Fall 1927 to Sept. 1928.

But he was still aware that the existence of a leisure class was essential to higher culture and that the Puritan conscience of America looked suspiciously upon leisure. For instance, he jotted this note in Vienna: "The Loafer is respected in Europe—he is not respected in America. All culture has at its bottom an art of loafing—often of loafing outwardly while undergoing the most terrible labor of the mind within. Work that is not visible and *profitable* is not recognized in America. Even a man with much money who desires to do nothing must develop a certain callousness—the atmosphere is not right. . . . But, despite this, over an equal period in recent time— viz. since 1910, I believe America has easily held its own creatively with Europe. The astonishing fact is that so much of what modern Europe has built with an eye to beauty is very ugly, and so much of what America has built with an eye to commerce is very beautiful." [4]

When he is away from America, he is quite homesick; his notes usually express it in physical terms, as when he says, "A man belongs to his country as an arm belongs to its socket. Any permanent separation from it is an amputation." [5] Sometimes he is childishly amusing in his nationalistic assertions. On a return voyage from Europe at one point he wrote, "America, I come. You are strong drink." [6] On another return voyage (with a number of Italian immigrants on board) he reveals his excitement as the ship approaches New York harbor in the morning: "Good feeling of a lucky day—the calm sea—the steady drive of the ship's motors . . . the feel of the mighty earth, the mighty city, of life beginning and awakening, the smoke and smell of 90 million breakfasts in the air . . . America still means Hope and Life to me. I am the True Immigrant. It means Youth. I am 28." [7] This idea of Hope, the American dream of opportunity, is not just something he mechanically worked into his novels. He really believed it. He remarked after some observations about the air of hopelessness in England in the 1930's: "I have heard Communists, friends I know in New York, talk gloatingly about our people sodden with despair, [muttering?] with revolution, living in a miserable degraded state of utter hopelessness—but by such foolishness

[4] PN 6, Nov. 1928 to Dec. 1928.
[5] PN 8, Dec. 1928 to Jan. 1929.
[6] PN 2, Nov. 1926 to Sept. 1927.
[7] PN 8.

they betray their ignorance, their feeble grasp, their failure to know anything about the country they are going to revolutionize—the American hope is fantastic, staggering, mad." [8]

In spite of the cultural chauvinism he expresses, the entries in his notebooks reveal a sense of cultural insecurity. The search for roots and for tradition is a common feature of American literary history, but Wolfe's concern, which is unusual for an American writer of his generation (i.e. one who was too young to be in World War I), shows a sense of responsibility about being a representative American writer. He jots down what he calls "an inquiry into the state of my culture" and considers what he knows about the literatures of Greece, Rome, France, Germany, England, and America.[9] He is very much aware of the European foundation for American culture. When he draws up "A Library for a Young Man of Today," he begins with Plato and Herodotus and comes up to Joyce and Mann— but there is not one American work on the list.[10] On his many European journeys he gluts himself on museums and exhausts his energy prowling through the bookshops. Sometimes he recognizes that he is displaying a kind of cultural megalomania. In 1928, he scribbles ". . . I am tired—the desire for it *all* comes from an evil gluttony in me—a weakness, a lack of belief." [11] But most of the time, he keeps up his intense pursuit of cultural strength as well as his pursuit of meaningful personal experiences. Note, for example, this passage which indicates his dedication at the end of one of his European voyages: "But deeper study always, sharper senses, profounder living. *Never* an end to curiosity! The fruit of all this comes later, I must think. I must mix it all with myself and with America. I have caught much of it on paper. But infinitely the greater part is in the wash of my brain and blood." [12]

But these are only manifestations of national awareness and a sense of cultural responsibility. They do not indicate a conscious purpose of giving expression to American life. The dedication to this literary goal developed only after Wolfe's first novel was published. Reviewers of *Look Homeward, Angel* had praised it and de-

[8] PN 26, Mar. 21, 1935, to *ca.* April 26, 1935.
[9] PN 5, Oct. 24, 1928, to Nov. 1928.
[10] PN 5.
[11] PN 5.
[12] PN 8.

clared that it was in the tradition of Melville and Whitman. That same year America's first Nobel Prize winner in literature, Sinclair Lewis, mentioned Wolfe's novel in his acceptance speech, pointing to it as evidence of the great promise of the American literature of the future. Wolfe felt a new responsibility: he had to live up to the best in the American literary tradition. But this sense of purpose was something he had been gradually becoming conscious of for some time.

When I mentioned earlier what Wolfe conceived to be the special problems of the American writer, I had in mind especially his frequently quoted statement at the end of *The Story of a Novel:*

> The life of the artist at any epoch of man's history has not been an easy one. And here in America, it has often seemed to me, it well may be the hardest that man has ever known. . . . It seems to me that the task [of the artist] is one whose physical proportions are vaster and more difficult here than in any other nation on the earth. It is not merely that in the cultures of Europe and the Orient the American artist can find no antecedent scheme, no structural plan, no body of tradition that can give his own work the validity and truth that it must have. It is not merely that he must make somehow a new tradition for himself, derived from his own life and from the enormous space and energy of American life . . . it is even more than this: that the labor of a complete and whole articulation, the discovery of an entire universe and of a complete language, is the task that lies before him.

> Such is the nature of the struggle to which henceforth our lives must be devoted. Out of the billion forms of America, out of the savage violence and the dense complexity of all its swarming life; from the unique and single substance of this land and life of ours, must we draw the power and energy of our own life, the articulation of our speech, the substance of our art.[13]

I have said in my book, *The Window of Memory,* that this problem of multiplicity and diversity of experience for the artist is not just an American problem—but that it is also an urban problem and a twentieth-century problem. But Wolfe saw it as an American problem, and he happened to be a twentieth-century American writer living in urban centers. He thought it was an American problem, and he set out to be an American spokesman: he set himself to cap-

[13] New York: Charles Scribner's Sons, 1936.

ture and subdue the multiplicity and diversity of American life.

Already he felt he represented some of this diversity in his own background and experience. His mother's people were Southerners long established in North Carolina; his father was a Northerner from Pennsylvania. Forebears on each side had shed blood in the Civil War. He was a Southerner, yet he came from the mountain area of western North Carolina, which was characteristic of another whole region. He had the small town experience of Asheville, North Carolina, but he spent his adult life in Boston and New York. The examples could be easily multiplied.

But it is in his notebooks that his sense of the multiplicity and diversity of American life appears in staggering evidence, for Wolfe had gradually begun to look upon his pocket notebook records as his own kind of research method.

I could try to categorize it—to say some of it is research into books, documents, records, some of it is deep-sea diving into his memory, and some of it is field research (observations of human behavior that he met in his travels, records of conversations he had with various people, and so on). But that would over-intellectualize and perhaps falsify what this activity is. What he is actually trying to do has varying purposes but is all intended to help him in writing his novels. What he is doing, for the most part, is attempting to set down fleeting words or impressions that came to his ear or eye as he roamed about, or trying to reel in elusive memories that swim up or to sort out a jumble of facts that are jostling each other in his mind. Let me give some examples.

Sometimes he records scraps of conversation overheard at lunch counters or in bars. One comes suddenly on a notebook entry like this:

So I says, That prick, that friend of yours owes me $150.00. When's he goin' to pay me?

So Johnny Sheehan says to me, he says, Any goddammed thing you want I'll do, he says.

So I says, Thass all rite.

So he says, Can you reach Bill Griffin? So he says, Yes—What did I start to tell you? Oh, I know—So he says to me one night, so he says to me, Do you know a fellow named Mike Marty?

So I looks at the son of a bitch and I says, Sure. So I says to him. . . .[14]

Once in a while, they are only brief statements that someone had dropped while Wolfe was passing by. Like these:

He must have money, though, somewhere.[15]

Now that my boss is gone, let's drink.[16]

They're a live bunch out there.[17]

Or what is obviously something overheard on a party line of the telephone:

Dintcha getcha potty?

No, I dint.

Oh 'm sawry. Ah'll connectcha up again.

Hello.

Hello—Is this extension 312?

That's it. You got it.

Now, I was speakin' to you a few minutes ago about a parcel.

Oh! *You're* the one! Dincha get that fellah?

No, I dint.

Well, I told 'm. Dincha speak to 'm?

No. I dint.

Someone musta cutcha off I guess.

Yes, Someone musta.

Well, you hold the wyeh. I'll go gettum for yuh.[18]

What he is after are records of American language and American speech patterns. Sometimes he only jots down the typical phrases

---

[14] PN 13, Feb. 1930 to May 1930. One entry in a notebook confirms the fact that he took down these conversations as he heard them. After one badly scribbled series of notes, he recorded: "I wrote this under the table because two people . . . across the room are watching me—with superior smiles and indecent curiosity." PN 13.

[15] PN 11, June 11, 1929, to Oct. 15, 1929.

[16] PN 13.

[17] PN 12, Oct. 1929 to Jan. 1930.

[18] PN 18, *ca.* Jan. 1932 to Aug. 1932.

and omits the subject matter of the conversation (the ellipsis marks
are all Wolfe's):

> Smartest guy in the world and they sold 'em as new . . . he says. I says
> . . . he says. . . . Bar none . . . he's the only boy in the world who
> thinks. . . . I don't give a damn what you think. . . . Bar none. He
> said How'd you find out. . . . I said How'd I find *out?* [19]

Occasionally he records a whole scene. Once he even woke up in
the middle of the night in Brooklyn and got out his pencil to set
down what he heard:

> 4:50 A.M. Sunday Morning, June 18 (?), 1931. First light just breaking—
> outside my windows on Verandah Place—low voices of several men in
> shirt sleeves pleading with woman to get up. Woman, fat, Irish-looking,
> has befouled herself.
>
> Get up now. Come on, get up. You ain't actin' like a lady, that's the trou-
> ble wit' you.
>
> O le' me go home.
>
> Not until you start actin' like a lady. Come on now (low persuasive voice)
> Get up. Start actin' like a lady.
>
> To hell wit' you! Lemme go home. O lemme go home.
>
> Start actin' like a lady. Get up. Get up.
>
> To hell wit' you. I wanna go home.
>
> Two other men: Aw, why can't you get a cab and take her home?
>
> Not until she starts actin' like a lady. I don't wanna take her home till
> she starts actin' like a lady.
>
> To hell wit you. Lemme go home.
>
> Don't talk like that. Start actin' like a lady.
>
> 4:55 o'clock. First light—first bird—wind in leaves—yesterday, a scorch-
> ing 93° heat struck—today prob. the same. [20]

Working with notes like these, Wolfe, is later able to produce
authentic American idiom for such pieces as "Only the Dead Know

---

[19] PN 13.

[20] The Good Child's River ledger 1, p. 244, Harvard Library. Wolfe later used
this incident in "No Door." See *From Death to Morning* (New York: Charles
Scribner's Sons, 1935) p. 10.

Brooklyn" or the "Voice of the City" passages in *Of Time and the River*.

In the same way he catches the city scene and the great variety of its actors by setting down notes of a particular occasion. One night on a subway going to Brooklyn at 3 A.M., he described all the passengers.[21] Another time in a kind of diary passage he records his own wandering and the mood created by what he saw: "Went to Lido—got pt. gin—went to Joe's, ate—walked to Atlantic Ave.—Rode to 4th Ave. on st. car—came back to Clark St. on Subway—drunk woman crying and weeping and accusing man of beating her —negro elevator boy says to cop above, 'Dere's a fight downstairs—a man's beatin' on a woman.' Cop runs into booth—gets gun and goes down. Horror! Horror! Horror!" [22]

More often he describes scenes when he is on his travels. They are usually unimportant scenes, but are characteristic of the place whether it be Germany or France, New Orleans or Hollywood. Here is one from Holland:

> Amsterdam, Mon., Feb. 1931, 4:30 P.M.—a grey wet wintery day full of rainspume and wetness—Coffee in Bodega at top of Kalver Straat (the main shopping street)—It is a small tortuous continental street crowded with shops and people—Here there are no motors but people wheel bicycles, and there is the single solid strangely lonely sound of thousands and thousands of men and women walking—the sound of shoe leather. Watched the great motor barges in canals—piled with fat filled sacks—children coming from school like children coming from school the world over—their bright shrill noises—The people go by under wet skies, many bear umbrellas, it is the 16th day of Feb. 1931 and now this is lost forever.[23]

Sometimes, he turns to written sources. He looks over newspapers. He is not interested in the principal events in the news; he is interested in the whole social scene. "What idea of modern life," he asks, "would a hermit get from [these newspapers]?" [24] When he jots down notes, they cover a great range of items. One set from the *New York Times*, May 2, 1932, contains a record of the weather and the tem-

[21] PN 22, *ca.* Apr. 1934 to July 1934.
[22] PN 18.
[23] PN 16, Feb. 16, 1931 to *ca.* Summer 1931.
[24] PN 6.

perature, notes on how May Day was observed by the workers of
the world, about some bloodshed in Poland over the May Day celebration, about Al Smith's victory in a California primary election,
about Macy's department store advertisements, about advertisements
for razor blades, for Squibbs Shaving Cream, about the circulation
figures for *Delineator* magazine, notes from the society page about
weddings, from the sports page about Babe Ruth and Jack Sharkey,
something about Trotsky and Stalin, something about Coolidge
going to the Circus to scrutinize a Sea Elephant.[25]

Then, of course, there are the lists and tabulations which are
abbreviations of his experience. At times this listing seems a kind
of lonely man's game or ritualistic conjuring up the past, as when
he sets down the names of people he knows best, or people he has
met on board ship on a particular voyage, or when he scribbles out
the names of cities in Central Europe that he has visited, or lists
of the States of U.S. he has entered. These lists are barren of comment. But at other times he will have some notations that give us
a clue as to what he is trying to do. One list of various family groups
he knows is headed "The Way Men Live" and he has noted their
sources of income, whether they are on relief or not, and a few
phrases—e.g. one family is described as "pale, sunless . . . they look
as if they have always lived in basements"; another, "a good family
gone to seed." [26]

At times his lists are clearly arranged for literary use. He set
down the deaths he had witnessed in New York and later developed
the notes into "Death the Proud Brother." [27] He searched his memory for incidents that could be accumulated for George Webber's
mental parade during a fit of insane jealousy. This list is entitled
simply *"Shame,"* and it reads as follows:

1) A Kid Slapped in The Face before his Girl.
2) A Manly-looking Man Humiliated Before His Mistress.
3) The Man In The North Station At Boston.
4) The Fight At the Dance.
5) The National Guard Kid in his Uniform.
6) The Jew On The Boat.

[25] PN 19, *ca.* Sept. 1932 to *ca.* Feb. 1933.
[26] PN 26.
[27] PN 18.

7) The Sailors On The Subway Car.

8) The woman and her lover at Nick's Grill.

[9] The Man Who Hit My Father In the Eye When He Was Drunk. For a Boy there is no more terrible thing than to see his father is afraid before another man. . . .[28]

In summary, one might say that notes like these indicate the means by which Wolfe made his work superior to the usual autobiographical fiction. He selected among the details and illustrations of life peripheral to his own and arranged them to convey the tone, the color, the richness of the American experience. The adventures of his central character are seen as only a part of a larger life. The experience becomes, then, not personal but national, and the literary mode becomes epic.

But Wolfe wanted also to reach back into the past to display the same kind of living social organism of the 1870's and 1880's. He wanted to create a milieu for Esther Jack and her father, Joe Linder, the characters based on Aline Bernstein and her father, Joseph Frankau, who was an actor on the New York stage in the late nineteenth century. Although Wolfe did not have his own experience to fall back on, he employed the same method. But he now had to depend on written records. The pocket notebooks indicate that Wolfe looked up in the old City Directories the addresses of Joseph Frankau and Theodore Bernstein and then went out to take a look at these houses and apartments. The notebooks show that he read through Percy MacKaye's biography of Steele MacKaye because Joseph Frankau's best role was in Steele MacKaye's *Hazel Kirke*. He thumbed through old copies of *Life,* the comic weekly, and of *Leslie's* illustrated magazine. He went through old issues of the *New York Times* taking notes which show the same kind of widespread interest with which he looked over the newspapers of the 1930's. Here is a sample of the variety of the notes:

Dec. 27 [1881]:
Clara Morris—to open in The New Magdalen at Union Sq. Theater.

Tues., Dec. 27:
Christmas celebrated on Monday—Dancing bands of ragamuffins tooting fifes in street—Christmas in Missions, Newsboys' lodging houses,

[28] PN 18.

etc.—Mrs. John Jacob Astor and Andrew Carnegie—crowds of carriages on Fifth Avenue.

Dec. 23, 1881:
Booth's Theater sold—to be made Dry Goods Store—price $550,000—opened Feb. 1869—Booth as Romeo.

Costumes of the Season—Sun. Dec. 25, 1881:
"Many fresh capotes are to be seen. The newest among these are of feathers. They are very small, with flat crowns covered with royal pheasants or 'lophophore'. On the brim is a full plush or velvet ruching harmonizing with the general coloring of feathers."

Dec. 20:
Death of Siro Delmonico.
Died Mon. Dec. 19 between 1 and two in morning at nephew Charles' house— On Sunday evening at Fifth Avenue and 26th St. Delmonico with party of friends—Later went to Brown's restaurant at midnight for supper—smoked 100 cigars a day.

New York Times, Dec. 27, 1881—Tuesday:
A Noble Porker's Death.
Christmas Hog-Guessing at Gabe Case's Club House (a saloon)—"a string of carriages formed under the horse sheds." "leaning over mahogany bar."
Guesses cost $1 apiece—Stoop of Hoboken Turtle Club House covered with spectators—an Italian 4-piece band playing away for dear life. The band played "I'm going home to die no more" as pig died. As Gabe Case awards prize (coming around corner), band plays "See the conquering hero comes." Case followed by judges, James Casey, clerk of the Gentlemen's Driving Ass'n, and Sam Sniffen—won by Frederick A. Ridaboch, the W. 54th St. Liveryman.

N. Y. Times, Dec. 26, 1881:
Mark Twain's speech in Philadelphia on the Pilgrims—Scenes of N. E. dinner—Fine. . . .
Guiteau—assassin of Garfield—Christmas in Jail in Washington—Eats Hearty Dinner.[29]

These are the evidences of the way Wolfe went about his task of rendering the multiplicity and variety and vitality of America both past and present.

But there was another American problem that he had to deal

[29] PN 16.

with successfully if he was to reflect the national life. There was another sort of multiplicity and diversity. There was the immense variety of human kind that made up the American nation, a diversity in national origin and religious difference as well as some wide cleavages of class and caste.

Critics and commentators exhibit conflicting opinions as to how satisfactorily Wolfe dealt with this area of the American experience in his novels. But one way or another, his notebooks confirm and even strengthen the evidence there in the novels that Wolfe was, for most of his career, narrow and intolerant of human diversity, fearful and suspicious of the stranger or the representative of the minority group. His anti-Semitism is already generally recognized. The anti-Semitism is something of a paradox because of his love for Mrs. Aline Bernstein. His pet name for her was "my Jew." "A radio-[gram] last night from my dear Jew," [30] he would note. But even the term of endearment indicates his consciousness of her as strange, different, other. More often, the notebook entries merely refer to her as "the Jew." "A letter from the Jew today," he states; "Will the Jew meet me?" he quiries. When he wonders about the future of their relationship, he asks, "What rut of life with the Jew now? Is this a new beginning or a final ending?" [31] In his love for her, he refers to "my Jewess-haunted blood." [32] It is also a paradox that he had an irrational scorn for Jewish women, regarding them as women who granted their sexual favors freely. For instance, one occasion when he saw a Jewish woman whom he knew come into a restaurant with a Japanese sculptor, he reacts with disgust as he speculates on their sexual relationship. He then adds an offensive comment that Jewish women merely follow the whims of fashion in sexual matters.[33]

His notebooks are also full of identifications of people as belonging to national or racial groups. A person is an Irishman or a Swede or a Dutchman, and so on. Frequently the references to these groups are slighting or even contemptuous. He is aware, too, that this is the American mixture. When he is sailing into New York

[30] PN 2.
[31] PN 2.
[32] PN 2.
[33] PN 13.

on that ship with the many immigrants and thinking about his country, we find his observation: "This boat too is American—this swarthy stew of Italians, Greeks, and God knows what other combinations—This morning they are 'spikking Englis' (How are yew, Mister, etc.) and going about in their new cheap American clothes." [34] A Negro is mostly termed a "nigger" when notebook entries take notice of him, although the notebooks also indicate that Wolfe was willing to cross the color line in sexual encounters in Europe.

It is clear that Wolfe found it harder to adapt to the human diversity in his country than to other kinds of variety in the American scene, and this troubles the epic presentation that he attempted. The mid-century reader can look at the incongruous panorama that he created from the "billion forms of America" in a work like *Of Time and the River,* and he can perceive with pleasure authentic, orderly units. But again and again he comes upon crude social attitudes that mar these impressions: "Abe would read Eugene one of these letters grinning widely with Kike delight," "a young Italian with grease-black hair sleeked back in faultless patent-leather pompadour, who talked to her, eyes leering and half-lidded," "the Greek from Cleveland with his cheap tan suit . . . and with his hairy, seamed and pitted night-time face, his swarthy eyes, his lowering finger-breadth of forehead," "a young Harlem negro and his saffron wench, togged to the nines in tan and lavender." [35] These are reflections of a limited America, a white-Anglo-Saxon-Protestant America with all of its ethnic suspicions and hostilities. These intrusions interfere with the epic tone, which cannot admit littleness of mind. Even in Wolfe's later work one seldom finds resolutions of the tensions between American ideals and realities which the epic view demands.

Part of the difficulty, no doubt, is due to Wolfe's easily disturbed neurotic condition. I said earlier that the notebooks give glimpses into the depths of Wolfe's psyche, and since he is so open and honest in his jottings, he does not block from view the ugly, murky recesses. But the notebooks also reveal, with the same openness, the marks of a fearful and suspicious personality. He is afraid of crowds,

[34] PN 8.
[35] (New York: Charles Scribner's Sons, 1935), pp. 465 and 596.

and since he spent most of his later years in New York City this "crowd neurosis," as Wolfe himself referred to it, displays itself in lashing out against city life. "The American city temper is cowardly, vicious, and cruel," he writes in a typical passage, "servile and cringing when it is powerless; arrogant and overbearing when it holds the reins. Never put a uniform on an American—not even for running an elevator. He can't stand it." [36] He talks to himself and reassures himself, "Hold yourself in, son. Hold your courage." In another passage he asks, "Why do I become so angry when people stare at me?" "Fear—Fear—like a cold oil around my heart—of what I do not know—Always carry in your heart the war on fear, fear, fear." [37] On a later occasion, he shows that sometimes it was a real struggle to control his life: "Being born, living, dying—and we waste ourselves on petty squabbles—I am now in such a mood that the littlest things possess and harrow my soul—the small imbecile triumphs of other people give me pain, and my own no pleasure at all. This is courage: to screw and rivet every jerking nerve together by the supremest effort of the will, to conquer the nausea around the heart, the weakness in the bowels. . . ." [38]

Since Wolfe had these neurotic fears, it is reassuring to see entries that indicate a grappling with his xenophobia or show intermittent successes in coming to terms with his fellow creatures. He said at one of the turning points in mid-career, "In this world—whether there is room for all kinds or not—we must make room if necessary. . . . We must observe and forbear to waste ourselves in futile antagonisms, jealousies, and hostilities. I am becoming more and more adjusted to my place in the world—what it may finally be I do not know, but I must build up out of chaos a strong sufficient inner life; otherwise I will be torn to pieces in the whirlpool of the world. It is not for me to say now 'Am I better than this or worse than that?' but 'Am I making use of myself to the best of my capacity?' . . . I must do this for myself—in this, at present, is my chiefest hope." [39]

At the end of his career, Wolfe reached a point where he could

---

[36] PN 3.
[37] PN 2.
[38] PN 13.
[39] PN 3.

write a piece like "The Promise of America," which combined his feeling about the American earth and his faith in the American dream of opportunity and included a vision of a Negro, a Jew, and a boy from the South, each of them addressed as brother, achieving their success in American life. He was perhaps on his way to overcoming his prejudices and accepting in human terms the deepest meaning of our motto "E Pluribus Unum."

Wolfe's notebooks tell us how he went about his task of rendering the American experience into literary form and also explain some of the peculiar features of the outcome. His works are encyclopedic because he sought to embrace the diversity of American life. But to recognize diversity is not to integrate all the diverse elements, and Wolfe was able only occasionally to achieve the integrity that we think of as artistic wholeness. His best work is his first novel. In later work his plans were so complex and his scope so broad that he did not accomplish what he wished before he died. Perhaps too, his difficulty in accepting the diversity of human life in America contributed to his artistic uncertainties. Whether he ever would have brought his mammoth work about George Webber under control or not we will never know. But we certainly must respect his aim and ambition to create an American prose epic. We should also feel some admiration for a writer who, beset with neurotic difficulties, was still able to marshal his energies sufficiently well to achieve a partial success in his epic attempt. It is not beyond hope that the publication of Wolfe's notebooks could suggest a method for some gifted contemporary of ours to reach a more complete success.

# "Introduction" to
## *The Short Novels of Thomas Wolfe*

### *by C. Hugh Holman*

To present a collection of the short novels of Thomas Wolfe will seem to many of his readers a quixotic or even a perverse act, for Wolfe exists in the popular fancy and even in the opinion of many of his most devoted admirers as the fury-driven author of a vast but incomplete saga of one man's pilgrimage on earth, a saga so formless that the term *novel* can be applied to its parts only with extreme caution and so monumental that it exploded the covers of four vast books in which its portions were imprisoned. Of the book upon which he embarked after *Look Homeward, Angel,* Wolfe wrote: "What I had to deal with was material which covered almost 150 years in history, demanded the action of more than 2000 characters, and would in its final design include almost every racial type and social class of American life." In a letter in 1932 he said, "The book on which I have been working for the last two or three years is not a volume but a library."

Much of the criticism of Wolfe's work has centered on its seemingly uncontrolled and formless exuberance, and it has become almost a critical truism that he possessed great talent but little control, a magnificent sense of language but a limited awareness of the demands of plot, a sensuous recall that was nearly total but an almost shocking unwillingness to subject his material to critical elision.

Yet, paradoxically, Thomas Wolfe produced some of his best work in the middle length of the short novel, the length between

15,000 and 40,000 words. Indeed, during the grueling years between the publication of his first novel in 1929 and *Of Time and the River* in 1935, his reputation was sustained and enriched by his short novels as much as it was by Sinclair Lewis's brief but telling praise for him as a "Gargantuan creature with great gusto for life" in his Nobel Prize address in 1930.

Wolfe's whole career was an endless search for a language and a form in which to communicate his vision of reality. "I believe with all my heart," he declared in *The Story of a Novel*, ". . . that each man for himself and in his own way . . . must find that way, that language, and that door—must find it for himself." This passion to find a mode of expression was coupled in Wolfe with a thoroughly organic view of art, one in which the thing to be said dictates the form in which it is uttered. He once wrote Hamilton Basso: "There is no accepted way: there are as many art forms as there are forms of art, and the artist will continue to create new ones and to enrich life with new creations as long as there is either life or art. So many of these forms that so many academic people consider as masterly and final definitions derived from the primeval source of all things beautiful or handed Apollo-wise from Mount Olympus, are really worn out already, will work no more, are already dead and stale as hell."

*Look Homeward, Angel* had almost automatically assumed a simple but effective narrative form. The record of childhood and youth, cast at least semi-consciously in the *bildungsroman* pattern of James Joyce's *A Portrait of the Artist as a Young Man,* had found its theme and taken its shape from the sequential flow of lyric feeling which it expressed. After its publication, Wolfe began a desperate search for another form into which to pour his materials. His letters between 1930 and 1934 are crowded with ambitious plans, nebulous projections of structure, plot, and myth, all pointed toward forming his next book. Increasingly its matter grew and the problems of the control of that matter enlarged.

By the fall of 1931 Wolfe found himself immersed in a struggle for form whose magnitude and difficulty, as well as spiritual and emotional anguish, he recorded touchingly in *The Story of a Novel.* In November, badly in need of money and in black despair over "the book," he turned to a body of materials in which he had earlier worked and began shaping them into a short novel. These materials dealt with his experiences in Cambridge and with his uncle, Henry Westall. In its finished form the short novel, *A Portrait of Bascom Hawke,* pictured an old man resigned to the death of dreams as he is seen through the eyes of a youth still half blinded by the visions of glory which the old man has given up. The two points of view, the youth's and the old man's, together gave a sense of the flow and corrosion of time. The result was a portrait in depth, done with irony, poignance, and tolerant laughter, of an eccentric who might have stepped from the pages of Dickens.

Fortunately, Wolfe had connections at this time with a publishing house which had a magazine, *Scribner's,* that was interested in the short novel as a literary form. Ludwig Lewisohn was generally correct when he asserted in 1932 that the short novel "is a form with which, in the English-speaking world, neither editors nor publishers seem ever to know what to do, trying to palm it off now as a short story and now as a novel." But in 1931 and 1932 *Scribner's Magazine* was publishing a novella in each issue, as a result of its second $5,000 Prize Short Novel contest, the announced aim of which was "to open up a field of fiction—the long-story field—which had been almost wholly neglected." In these contests, the best entries were published as they were received, and the prize was awarded to the best novel from both the published and unpublished entries. The characteristics of the short novels *Scribner's* was seeking were declared to be "adequate space for the development of character and setting, combined with precision and solidity of structure." The magazine had begun publishing short novels with James Gould Cozzen's "*S. S. San Pedro*" in August, 1930, the first of twelve long stories published as part of the first Prize Contest. Among the others were long tales by W. R. Burnett, André Maurois, and Marjorie Kinnan Rawlings. The contest was won by John Peale Bishop's *Many Thousands Gone.*

When Wolfe submitted *A Portrait of Bascom Hawke* to Maxwell Perkins in January, 1932, the second Prize Contest was nearing its February 1 closing date. Among the nine short novels published as a part of the second contest, in addition to *A Portrait of Bascom Hawke,* were long tales by Sherwood Anderson, Edith Wharton, and Katherine Anne Porter. The judges—Burton Rascoe, William

Soskin, and Edmund Wilson—declared the contest to be a tie between John Herrmann's *The Big Short Trip* and Wolfe's short novel, which was published in the April, 1932, issue of the magazine. Wolfe and Herrmann divided the $5,000 Prize between them.

*A Portrait of Bascom Hawke* gained considerable critical praise, such as that which Laurence Stallings gave it in *The New York Sun,* where he wrote: "Has anyone failed to admire a story in the *Scribner's Magazine* (for April) by Thomas Wolfe? There's an eddy of energy for you; and a lyrical paean to life. . . . It seems to me that Thomas Wolfe has shown in this story that his *October Fair,* announced for next fall, will be even finer than . . . *Look Homeward, Angel.* . . . He seems to have all the gifts, all the talents . . . 'A Portrait of Bascom Hawke' is the book of the month."

Apparently Wolfe had been ignorant of the existence of the Short Novel Contest until he submitted *A Portrait* to Perkins in January. Learning of the contest he resolved to write another novel to enter in it, despite the fact that less than a month remained before the contest ended. It was actually Perkins who entered *A Portrait of Bascom Hawke* in the contest which it won.

As his intended entry Wolfe set to work on a short novel fashioned on his mother's endless stories of the past. During the month of January she visited him in Brooklyn, and the immediate source of *The Web of Earth* was almost certainly her conversations. The Short Novel Contest had been over more than a month before the story was finished, but *Scribner's* promptly purchased it and published it in the July, 1932, issue.

This novella, the longest of Wolfe's short novels, comes to the reader entirely through the voice of its narrator, Delia Hawke (later changed to Eliza Gant when the novel was reprinted in *From Death to Morning*). Wolfe insisted, "It is different from anything I have ever done," and added, "that story about the old woman has got everything in it, murder and cruelty, and hate and love, and greed and enormous unconscious courage, yet the whole thing is told with the stark innocence of a child." The seemingly disparate elements of the story—disjointed in temporal and logical sequence—are effectively knit together by the powerful personality of the narrator and by her obsessive search in the events of her life for the meaning of the spectral voices that spoke "Two . . . Two" and "Twenty . . . Twenty" in "the year that the locusts came."

In writing *The Web of Earth* Wolfe followed James Joyce again, as he had done in *Look Homeward, Angel.* He compared his "old woman" with Molly Bloom and seemingly felt that his short novel had a structure like that of the interior monologue at the conclusion of *Ulysses.* In her resilience, her undefeatable energy, and her vitality Eliza (or Delia) approaches "the earth goddess" and is, as Louis D. Rubin, Jr. has pointed out, reminiscent of the end of the "Anna Livia Plurabelle" sequence of *Finnegans Wake,* a sequence which was published in the little magazine *transition* about the same time. In this short novel one understands what Wolfe meant when he referred to Eliza Gant's people as "time-devouring." Thus, *The Web of Earth* becomes a fascinating counterpiece to *A Portrait of Bascom Hawke;* for each is a character sketch of an elderly person, but where Bascom Hawke is defeated and despairingly resigned, Eliza Gant is triumphant and dominant; where Bascom is the male victim of time, Eliza is the female devourer of time; where Bascom's is the vain grasp of intellect and reason in a mad and fury-driven world, Eliza's is the groping of mystery, passion, and fear in a world where reason always falls victim to the decay of time. Never did Wolfe articulate more effectively than in these two short novels the fundamental polarities of his childhood and youth.

With these two short novels successfully behind him, Wolfe next turned to organizing into short novel form blocks of the material which he had written for the still formless "big book." In the period between March, 1933, and March, 1934, he put together four long stories or short novels from these materials, finding in the limits of the novella a means of focusing matter whose organization in larger blocks still defied him.

*Scribner's Magazine* bought three of these long tales and published them in successive issues in the summer of 1934. "The Train and the City," a long short-story of 12,000 words, appeared in the May issue. Percy MacKaye praised this story highly, still, it lacks the unity which Wolfe had achieved in his first two short novels. *Death the Proud Brother* appeared in the June issue, and was later republished as a short novel in *From Death to Morning.* This story

of 22,000 words was a skillfull attempt to unify a group of seemingly disparate incidents in the city through their common themes
of loneliness and death, "the proud brother of loneliness." Wolfe
regarded this story very highly, saying, "It represents *important*
work to me," and his novelist friend Robert Raynolds praised it
highly. Although it is a successful effort to impose thematic unity
upon disconnected instances of death in the city, it is less effective
than Wolfe's other novellas.

The third long story was *No Door,* in its original form a short
novel of 31,000 words, although it was published by *Scribner's* as
two long stories, "No Door" in July, 1933, and "The House of the
Far and the Lost" in August, 1934. In arranging the materials of
this novel. Wolfe selected a group of intensely autobiographical
incidents all centering on his sense of incommunicable loneliness
and insularity, dislocated them in time, and bound them together
by a group of recurring symbols arranged in *leitmotif* patterns,
extending and enriching a method he had used in *Death the Proud
Brother.* Through the recurring images and the repeated phrases
of a prose poem used as a prologue, he knit together one portion of
his life. In its concluding episode are united the themes of youth's
exuberance and age's sad wisdom, which had been central to *A Portrait of Bascom Hawke,* and the enduring earth, which had been
central to *The Web of Earth.*

It was in the early months of 1933 that *No Door* was completed,
and by March it had been accepted by *Scribner's.* Its completion
coincided with Wolfe's discovery of a plan which made work on
the "big book" feasible for him again. He wrote to George Wallace:
". . . just after you left in January . . . I plunged into work and
. . . I seemed suddenly to get what I had been trying to get for two
years, the way to begin the book, and make it flow, and now it is all
coming with a rush." Since the structure of *No Door* is essentially
that of *Of Time and the River,* since the prologue to *No Door* reappears with only minor changes as the prologue to the long novel,
and since the writing of *No Door* coincides with the finding of a
"way to begin the book," it is probable that the short novel was the
door through which Wolfe entered *Of Time and the River.* John
Hall Wheelock praised *No Door* highly, and Maxwell Perkins

agreed to bring out a limited edition of the short novel in its original form. However, its absorption into *Of Time and the River* was almost complete, and it seemingly has survived as a unit only in the form of its brief first incident, published as a short story in *From Death to Morning,* where it achieved notoriety as the basis for a libel suit brought against Wolfe and Scribner's by Marjorie Dorman and her family in 1936.

Yet *No Door* represents as sure a mastery as Wolfe ever demonstrated of the subjective, autobiographical materials for which he is best known. Of the section published as "The House of the Far and the Lost," Robert Penn Warren wrote in a review almost brutally unsympathetic to *Of Time and the River*: "Only in the section dealing with the Coulson episode does Mr. Wolfe seem to have all his resources for character presentation under control. The men who room in the house . . . with the Coulsons themselves are very precise to the imagination, and are sketched in with an economy usually foreign to Mr. Wolfe. . . . Here Mr. Wolfe has managed to convey an atmosphere and to convince the reader of the reality of his characters without any of his habitual exaggerations of method and style. This section . . . possesses what is rare enough in *Of Time and the River,* a constant focus." The Coulson episode is clearly the most striking one in *No Door.* It is also an integral part of that work, and the entire short novel possesses the strong virtues that Mr. Warren here assigns to the only portion of it which survived as a unified part of the long novel.

One other short novel resulted from Wolfe's arranging of materials from the "big book" during this period. It was *Boom Town,* a story of approximately 20,000 words, portraying the real estate craze in Asheville in the satiric manner of Sinclair Lewis. This short novel was published in the *American Mercury* in May, 1934, but it had been written before *No Door.*

The discovery of an organizing principle for the "big book" brought a temporary end to Wolfe's work in the short novel form; for the next two years he devoted himself single-mindedly to *Of Time and the River.* Thus during his first period—the one of which he said, "I began to write with an intense and passionate concern with the designs and purposes of my own youth"—Thomas

Wolfe produced, in addition to his two long novels, five short ones: *A Portrait of Bascom Hawke, The Web of Earth, Death the Proud Brother, Boom Town,* and *No Door*. These short novels helped to sustain his reputation, demonstrated his artistry and control of his materials, and perhaps instructed his sense of form.

When he entered the second period of his career—that of which he said, "[My] preoccupation [with my own youth] has now changed to an intense and passionate concern with the designs and purposes of life"—he found himself once more facing the problem of finding a new and adequate form in which to express his vision of experience. This search for an organic structure was complicated by his growing difficulties with his publishers and his increasing unwillingness to follow the advice of his editor, Maxwell E. Perkins. In this situation, in some respects like that of 1931, Wolfe turned his attention again to elements of his experience that lent themselves to expression in the short novel form.

In the summer of 1936 he made his last visit to Germany, a nation that he loved and that had heaped adulation upon him. On this trip he was forced to face the frightening substratum of Naziism, what he called "a picture of the Dark Ages come again—shocking beyond belief, but true as the hell that man forever creates for himself." And he said, "I recognized at last, in all its frightful aspects, the spiritual disease which was poisoning unto death a noble and mighty people." That fall he used the short novel form to dramatize this perception of the truth about Hitler's Germany, and he elected to give his account, which he entitled *"I Have a Thing to Tell You,"* the sharp intensity and the almost stark directness of the action story. At this time Wolfe had great admiration for the directness and simplicity of Ernest Hemingway's style, and in this short novel of Germany he came closest to adopting some of its characteristics. Nothing Wolfe ever wrote has greater narrative drive or more straightforward action than this novella. The simplicity and objectivity of *"I Have a Thing to Tell You"* were seldom sustained for any length of time in Wolfe's work before 1936.

This short novel also displays clearly the growing concern with the issues of the outer world which had begun to shape Wolfe's thinking. Its publication in the *New Republic* as a serial in March, 1937, despite his disclaimers of propaganda intent, indicates a marked advance in the expression of political and social concerns for Wolfe.

During much of 1937, Wolfe's energies were expended in his long and tortuous break with his publishers, Charles Scribner's Sons, certainly one of the two major emotional cataclysms of his life (the other was his earlier break with his mistress, Aline Bernstein). He was also deeply discouraged about his projected book, feeling that his long-planned and talked-of *October Fair,* often announced, was somehow being dissipated in fragments. In this despairing state, he was led by his growing sense of social injustice to attempt another experiment with a short novel as a vehicle of social criticism. He worked on this new novella, *The Party at Jack's,* during the early months of the year and spent the summer in revising and rewriting it.

Wolfe felt that he was attempting in *The Party at Jack's* "one of the most curious and difficult problems that I have been faced with in a long time," the presentation of a cross-section of society through a representation of many people, ranging from policemen, servants, and entertainers to the leaders in the literary world and the rich in the events of a single evening during which they were brought together through a party and a fire in the apartment house in which the party occurred. He used several devices, including the recurring quivering of the apartment house as the trains run in tunnels through its seemingly solid rock foundations and the conversations of the doormen and elevator operators, to underscore the contrast among the characters and to comment on society. Wolfe feared that readers would think this short novel to be Marxist, a charge against which he defended it, saying: ". . . there is not a word of propaganda in it. It is certainly not at all Marxian, but it is representative of the way my life has come—after deep feeling, deep thinking, and deep living and all this experience—to take its way. . . . It is in concept, at any rate, the most densely woven piece of writing that I have ever attempted."

*The Party at Jack's* is, as Wolfe asserted, free of autobiography, except in the most incidental ways. It is also in Wolfe's late, more economical style. Its taut prose and its rapid movement, together with its effective but implicit statement of social doctrine, make it one of Wolfe's most impressive accomplishments.

Almost immediately after completing *The Party at Jack's,* Wolfe plunged into the organizing of his materials into another "big book" for his new publishers, Harper and Brothers, a task which he was prevented from completing by his death in September, 1938. He had written—in addition to a mass of manuscript out of which three later books were assembled—two novels, a number of short stories, and seven short novels.

Upon these seven short novels Wolfe had expended great effort, and in them he had given the clearest demonstrations he ever made of his craftsmanship and his artistic control. Each of these seven novellas is marked in its unique way by a sharp focus and a controlling unity, and each represents a serious experiment with form. Yet they have virtually been lost from the corpus of Wolfe's work, lost even to most of those who know that work well.

There were two reasons for these losses. In the first place Wolfe's publishers, and particularly his editor, Maxwell E. Perkins, were anxious that the long, introspective *Look Homeward, Angel* be followed by an equally impressive work. Perkins urged Wolfe to continue the Eugene Gant story and discouraged his coming before the public in a different form or manner. Wolfe at one time wanted *Look Homeward, Angel* to be followed by *No Door,* a work of less than 40,000 words, and that small book might have been followed by a volume which Wolfe described to his mother that would contain *A Portrait of Bascom Hawke, The Web of Earth,* and "another story which [he had] written," probably "The Train and the City." At this time, however, Wolfe was happy to rely on his editor's judgment, and did not trust his own.

A second reason for the loss of these short novels is the nature of Wolfe's work and his attitude toward it. All the separate parts of his writing formed for him portions of a great and eternally fragmentary whole. It was all the outgrowth of the same basic desire, the Whitmanesque attempt to put a person on record and through that person to represent America in its paradox of unity and variety, at the same time employing as his essential theme the eternal and intolerable loneliness of the individual lost in the complex currents of time. As a result, Wolfe was forever reshuffling the parts of his work and assembling them in different patterns, in a way not unlike the shifting elements of the Snopes material in Faulkner's continuing legend of Yoknapatawpha County. Thus Wolfe took the materials he had presented first as short novels and interwove them into the larger frames and subject matters of his "big books," fragmenting, expanding, and modifying them, and often destroying their separate integrity. Only two of his short novels escaped this process; and these two—*Death the Proud Brother* and *The Web of Earth*—were published in a collection of his shorter works, *From Death to Morning*, which has never received the critical attention that it deserves.

In his short novels Wolfe was dealing with limited aspects of experience, aspects that could be adequately developed in the limits of 15,000 to 40,000 words and that could be organized into what he proudly called *The Party at Jack's*, "a single thing." When later he fragmented these short novels and distributed the fragments within the larger design of the "big books," he robbed them of their own unity in order to make them a portion of a larger and more complex unity—"a single thing" of complex and multifarious parts. Indeed, Wolfe's treatment of his short novels when he incorporated them later into his long books (and there is no reason to doubt that he would have approved the use made by his editor of the longer versions of *"I Have a Thing to Tell You"* and *The Party at Jack's* in *You Can't Go Home Again*) is a key to one of Wolfe's central problems, the finding of a large form sufficient to unify his massive imaginative picture of experience. This large form that he sought would give, apparently, not the representation of a series of sharply realized dramatic moments in the life of his protagonist (and through him of America) but an actual and significant interweaving of these moments into a complex fabric of event, time, and feeling. That he struggled unceasingly for the mastery of this vast structure is obvious from his letters, from *The Story of a Novel*, and from the long books themselves. Whether he was moving toward its realization is a matter of critical debate today, as it was at the time of his death. However much one may feel that he was (and I share that belief), the fact remains that none of the published novels after

*Look Homeward, Angel* succeeded in finding a clearly demonstrable unity, in being "a single thing."

The intrinsic qualities of the short novel were remarkably well adapted to Wolfe's special talents and creative methods. Although he was skilled at the revelatory vignette, in which he imprisoned a character in an instance in time, those characters and actions which were central to his effort and experience he saw in relation to the expanding pattern of life. Experience and life itself were for him, as Herbert Muller has noted, remarkably "in process." One of the distinctive aspects of Wolfe's imagination is its tendency to see life as a thing of "becoming." He saw time—"dark time," he called it —as being at the center of the mystery of experience, and its representation on three complex levels was a major concern of his work. The individual scene or person had little value to him; it had to be put back in time to assume meaning. Wolfe was very explicit about this element of his work. In *The Story of a Novel* he says: "All of this time I was being baffled by a certain time element in the book, by a time relation which could not be escaped, and for which I was now desperately seeking some structural channel. There were three time elements inherent in the material. The first and most obvious was an element of actual present time, an element which carried the narrative forward, which represented characters and events as living in the present and moving forward into an immediate future. The second time element was of past time, one which represented these same characters as acting and as being acted upon by all the accumulated impact of man's experience so that each moment of their lives was conditioned not only by what they experienced in that moment, but by all that they had experienced up to that moment. In addition to these two time elements, there was a third which I conceived as being time immutable, the time of rivers, mountains, oceans, and the earth; a kind of eternal and unchanging universe of time against which would be projected the transcience of man's life, the bitter briefness of his day. It was the tremendous problem of these three time elements that almost defeated me and that cost me countless hours of anguish in the years that were to follow."

Ultimately in the portrayal of an incident or an individual against this complex pattern of time, that incident or individual must be seen through a perceiving and remembering self, such as

David Hawke, the youth who can read the corrosion of time in the contrast between his exuberance and his uncle's resignation, in *A Portrait of Bascom Hawke*. Eliza Gant's fabric of memories in *The Web of Earth* is a record of the impact of time on her. The individual incidents of *No Door* assume their importance as portions of a personal history as they are reflected in the narrator's memory. To be fully understood, such events and people must be set against the innumerable other events and people which the perceiving self has known; it is this larger context in time which Wolfe attempts to give these short novels when he incorporates them in his longer works. We can think of an event as being an objective experience which is perceived and recalled later by the self that first knew it directly; then it, as fact and as memory, becomes a part of the totality of experience that makes the web of meaning for that self. Wolfe's short novels represent that portion of the process in which the incident is remembered, isolated, organized, and understood as incident by the self. Their later fragmentation and inclusion in the long novels represent his attempt to absorb them into his total experience and to use them in all the complexity of life as elements in his search for ultimate meaning. Hence he breaks up the sequence of actions, introduces new incidents, and frequently expands the wordage of the short novels when they are incorporated into the larger structures. These incidents thereby lose some of their artistic and inherent right to achieve unity by exclusion, and they tend to become diffuse.

Since Wolfe's success in achieving the larger unity for which he strove in the last three long novels is considerably less than total, the materials which he had organized into short novels have an integrity and a consummate craftsmanship which they seem to lack in the long books. It is for this reason that we are justified in reprinting here the five best short novels of Thomas Wolfe in the form in which he prepared them for magazine publication. In the short novel form Wolfe was a master of his craft, and these successful products of his efforts should not be forgotten.

# Chronology of Important Dates

| | |
|---|---|
| 1900 | Born October 3, Asheville, North Carolina |
| 1904 | Grover Cleveland Wolfe, brother, dies at St. Louis World's Fair |
| 1906 | Julia Elizabeth Wolfe buys Old Kentucky Home |
| 1912 | Enters North State Fitting School |
| 1916 | Enters University of North Carolina |
| 1918 | Works in Norfolk, Va., during summer; Benjamin Harrison Wolfe, brother, dies |
| 1920 | Enters graduate school at Harvard University |
| 1922 | William Oliver Wolfe, father, dies |
| 1923 | Play, *Welcome to Our City*, staged by '47 Workshop |
| 1924 | Accepts teaching position at New York University; first trip to Europe |
| 1925 | Meets Aline Bernstein |
| 1926 | Goes abroad with Aline Bernstein; begins novel |
| 1927 | Goes abroad with Aline Bernstein |
| 1928 | Completes manuscript of *Look Homeward, Angel*; rift with Aline Bernstein; Scribner's expresses interest in novel |
| 1929 | "The Angel on the Porch" published in *Scribner's Magazine*; *Look Homeward, Angel* published |
| 1930 | Ends teaching job at N. Y. U.; awarded Guggenheim Fellowship; goes abroad |
| 1931 | Aline Bernstein attempts suicide |

1932    Definitive break with Aline Bernstein; *A Portrait of Bascom Hawke*

1934    *Of Time and the River* sent to printer

1935    *Of Time and the River;* visits Germany; *From Death to Morning*

1936    *The Story of a Novel;* visits Germany

1937    "I Have a Thing to Tell You"; visits Asheville for first time since 1929; signs contract with Harper's

1938    Tours national parks; ill with pneumonia in Seattle, Washington; operated on at Johns Hopkins Hospital; dies Baltimore, September 15; buried in Asheville

1939    *The Web and the Rock*

1940    *You Can't Go Home Again*

1941    *The Hills Beyond*

1943    *Thomas Wolfe's Letters to His Mother*

1945    Julia Elizabeth Wolfe dies

1948    *Mannerhouse*

1951    *A Western Journal*

1956    *The Letters of Thomas Wolfe*

1961    *The Short Novels of Thomas Wolfe*

1971    *The Notebooks of Thomas Wolfe*

# Notes on the Editor and Contributors

Louis D. Rubin, Jr., the editor of this volume in the Twentieth Century Views series, is Professor of English in the University of North Carolina at Chapel Hill. He is author of *Thomas Wolfe: The Weather of His Youth* (1955), *The Faraway Country: Writers of the Modern South* (1963), *The Teller in the Tale* (1967), *George W. Cable: the Life and Times of a Southern Heretic* (1969), *The Writer in the South* (1972), and numerous other books on American literature, as well as a novel, *The Golden Weather* (1961).

Morris Beja, Professor of English at Ohio State University, is author of *Epiphany in the Modern Novel* (1971), which contains an expanded version of the essay in this collection, and various essays on British and American fiction. He has been Fulbright lecturer at the University of Thessaloniki, Greece.

John Peale Bishop (1892–1944), a native of Charles Town, West Virginia, was a poet, novelist and critic. His works of fiction include *Many Thousands Gone* (1931) and *Act of Darkness* (1935). His *Collected Poems* were edited by Allen Tate (1948) and his *Collected Essays* by Edmund Wilson (1948).

Bernard DeVoto (1897–1955) was critic, journalist, novelist and historian. From 1936 to 1938 he edited the *Saturday Review of Literature,* and from 1935 until his death he wrote the *Editor's Easy Chair* department of *Harper's Magazine.* Among his many books are *Mark Twain's America* (1932), *The World of Fiction* (1950), *The Year of Decision: 1848* (1943), *Across the Wide Missouri* (1947) and *The Course of Empire* (1952).

Wilbur M. Frohock is author of *The Novel of Violence in America* (1950), *André Malraux and the Tragic Imagination* (1952), *Strangers to the Ground* (1962) and *Rimbaud's Poetic Practice* (1963). He is Professor of Romance Languages at Harvard University.

C. Hugh Holman is Kenan Professor of English at the University of North Carolina at Chapel Hill. His books include *A Handbook to Literature* (1971), *Three Modes of Southern Fiction* (1966) and *The Roots of Southern*

*Writing* (1972). He has edited *The Short Novels of Thomas Wolfe* (1961), *The World of Thomas Wolfe* (1962), *The Thomas Wolfe Reader* (1962), and, with Sue Fields Ross, *The Letters of Thomas Wolfe to His Mother* (1968). A volume of his essays on Wolfe will soon be published by the Louisiana State University Press.

PAMELA HANSFORD JOHNSON, wife of Sir Charles P. Snow, is a British novelist and essayist of distinction. Her book on Thomas Wolfe was published in England as *Thomas Wolfe: A Critical Study* (1947) and in the United States as *Hungrey Gulliver: An English Appraisal of Thomas Wolfe* (1958), and reprinted with a new preface as *The Art of Thomas Wolfe* (1963).

ALFRED KAZIN, Professor of English at the State University of New York, Stony Brook, is author of *On Native Grounds: An Interpretation of American Prose Fiction* (1942), *The Inmost Leaf* (1955), *Contemporaries* (1962), and two autobiographical volumes, *A Walker in the City* (1951) and *Starting Out in the Thirties* (1965).

RICHARD S. KENNEDY is Professor of English at Temple University. He is author of *The Window of Memory: The Literary Career of Thomas Wolfe* (1962) and editor, with Paschal Reeves, of *The Notebooks of Thomas Wolfe* (1970). He has also written a number of articles on Wolfe and his fiction.

MAXWELL EWARTS PERKINS (1884–1947), was Thomas Wolfe's editor at Charles Scribner's Sons. One of the leading editors of his generation, he welcomed to Scribner's such writers as F. Scott Fitzgerald, Ernest Hemingway, and Ring Lardner. *Editor to Author: The Letters of Maxwell E. Perkins* was published in 1950.

WRIGHT MORRIS is author of numerous novels, including *My Uncle Dudley* (1942), *The Man Who Was There* (1945), *The Home Place* (1948), *Field of Vision* (1956), *Love Among the Cannibals* (1957), *Ceremony in Lone Tree* (1960) and *In Orbit* (1967). His study of the American literary imagination, *The Territory Ahead,* was published in 1958.

THOMAS C. MOSER is Professor of English at Stanford University. He is author of *Joseph Conrad: Achievement and Decline* (1957), has edited critical editions of *Wuthering Heights* and *Lord Jim,* and his written articles on Wolfe and others.

WILLIAM STYRON has written *Lie Down in Darkness* (1951), *The Long March* (1952), *Set This House On Fire* (1960), and *The Confessions of Nat Turner* (1967), novels which have placed him among the leading writers of fiction of his time.

# Bibliographical Note

The bibliographical essay by C. Hugh Holman in Jackson R. Bryer ed., *Fifteen Modern American Authors: a Survey of Research and Criticism* (Durham, N. C.: Duke University Press, 1969), is the most reliable guide to scholarship on Thomas Wolfe.

There are two biographies, both of them useful: Elizabeth Nowell, *Thomas Wolfe: A Biography* (Garden City, N. Y.: Doubleday and Co., 1960), and Andrew Turnbull, *Thomas Wolfe* (New York: Charles Scribner's Sons, 1968).

The single most important and useful work of scholarship on Wolfe is Richard S. Kennedy, *The Window of Memory: The Literary Career of Thomas Wolfe* (Chapel Hill: University of North Carolina Press, 1962). Other good book-length studies are Paschal Reeves, *Thomas Wolfe's Albatross: Race and Nationality in America* (Athens: University of Georgia Press, 1968), and Floyd C. Watkins, *Thomas Wolfe's Characters: Portraits from Life* (Norman: University of Oklahoma Press, 1959).

Full-length critical studies include two general introductory volumes, Bruce R. McElderry, Jr., *Thomas Wolfe* (New York: Twayne Publishers, 1964), and Richard Walser, *Thomas Wolfe: An Introduction and Interpretation* (New York: Barnes and Noble, 1961); and several works of critical analysis, Herbert J. Muller, *Thomas Wolfe* (Norfolk, Conn.: New Directions, 1947), Pamela Hansford Johnson, *The Art of Thomas Wolfe* (New York: Charles Scribner's Sons, 1963), and Louis D. Rubin, Jr., *Thomas Wolfe: The Weather of His Youth* (Baton Rouge: Louisiana State University Press, 1955).

88527

**DATE DUE**

| | | | |
|---|---|---|---|
| | | | |
| | | | |
| | | | |
| | | | |
| | | | |
| | | | |
| | | | |
| | | | |
| | | | |
| | | | |
| | | | |